THE
HEALING
Anointing

THE

HEALING
Anointing

Kenneth E. Hagin

Unless otherwise indicated, all scripture quotations are taken from the *King James Version* of the Bible.

25 24 23 22 21 20 19   18 17 16 15 14 13 12

The Healing Anointing
ISBN-13: 978-0-89276-527-0
ISBN-10: 0-89276-527-5

In the U.S. write:
Kenneth Hagin Ministries
P.O. Box 50126
Tulsa, OK 74150-0126
1-888-28-FAITH
rhema.org

In Canada write:
Kenneth Hagin Ministries of Canada
P.O. Box 335, Station D
Etobicoke (Toronto), Ontario
Canada M9A 4X3
1-866-70-RHEMA
rhemacanada.org

CONTENTS

—Chapter 1—

ASPECTS OF THE ANOINTING

And it shall come to pass in that day, that his BURDEN SHALL BE TAKEN AWAY from off thy shoulder, and his yoke from off thy neck, and THE YOKE SHALL BE DESTROYED because of the ANOINTING.

—Isaiah 10:27

And Jesus returned IN THE POWER OF THE SPIRIT into Galilee: and there went out a fame of him through all the region round about.

And he taught in their synagogues, being glorified of all.

And he came to Nazareth, where he had been brought up: and, as his custom was, he went into the synagogue on the sabbath day, and stood up for to read.

And there was delivered unto him the book of the prophet Esaias. And when he had opened the book, he found the place where it was written,

THE SPIRIT OF THE LORD IS UPON ME, because he hath ANOINTED me to preach the gospel to the poor; he hath sent me to HEAL the brokenhearted, to PREACH DELIVERANCE to the captives, AND RECOVERING OF SIGHT to the blind, to SET AT LIBERTY them that are bruised,

To preach the acceptable year of the Lord.

—Luke 4:14–19

Over the course of my ministry, I've spoken many times about different aspects of the anointing. Often the Lord will speak to me about something as I'm sitting on the platform getting ready to minister. I always carry some notecards or paper in my Bible so I can write down what He says to me. (If you don't write down what the Lord tells you, many times you'll let what He tells you get away from you.)

Once as I was sitting on the platform getting ready to minister, the Lord said to me, "Study further about the anointing." In obedience to the Lord, I began to study further on the subject. And since then, many times as I speak on the anointing, I get fresh revelation. Charles Spurgeon once said that no minister can really preach a sermon like it ought to be preached until he's preached it at least fifty times!

I know exactly what he was talking about! For example, I've been teaching on the subject of faith for over sixty years—more than half a century. But even though I've been teaching on faith all this time, almost every time I teach on it, I get fresh revelation. In other words, I see something I didn't see before.

You see, we never come to the place where we know it all. If we did ever come to that place, we would know as much as God, and that's just not possible! So thank God for the Word and for the anointing that teach us. Thank God for the privilege to study the Word.

THE ANOINTING DEFINED

Notice in one of our texts the words "Spirit" and "anointed" that are used in connection with the anointing.

LUKE 4:18-19

18 The SPIRIT OF THE LORD is upon me [Jesus], because he hath ANOINTED me [anointed Him to do what?] to preach the gospel to the poor; he hath sent me to heal the brokenhearted, to preach deliverance to the captives, and recovering of sight to the blind, to set at liberty them that are bruised,

19 To preach the acceptable year of the Lord.

Now look at Acts 10:38 and notice that "the Spirit of the Lord," "the anointing," "the Holy Ghost," and "power" are all synonymous terms.

ACTS 10:38

38 How God ANOINTED Jesus of Nazareth with the HOLY GHOST [the Spirit of the Lord] and with POWER: who went about doing good, and healing all that were oppressed of the devil; for God was with him.

Now the anointing can be an individual anointing or a corporate anointing.[1] Concerning the individual anointing, we know that God anoints individuals to minister. There are different offices in which God calls them to minister—the offices of the apostle, prophet, evangelist, pastor, and teacher. Jesus stood in all five of them, so He had the anointing that goes with every office.

Jesus had the anointing *without measure* (John 3:34). Members of the Body of Christ have the anointing *in a measure*. In other words, an individual only has the anointing that goes with the ministry office to which he's called.

I think about the different times during my field ministry when I've preached in churches and I'd see people coming to the pastors for help. I had been in the ministry quite a few years, and sometimes while I was sitting in the next room, I could hear the pastor counseling someone. I'd think, "This pastor is just a young man. He doesn't have one-tenth of the experience that I have in the ministry. How is he ever going to answer that question?"

Yet as I sat there and listened to him talk, the words that poured out of his mouth were full of wisdom and grace. Why? Because he had the anointing to stand in that office, the office of the pastor.

At one church where I was ministering, someone came to the local pastor for help while I was present. When this person told the pastor his problem, I remember thinking, "How is this pastor going to handle that? What is he going to do?"

When I heard how he ministered to that person, I wept. This pastor had an anointing to minister to that person that I didn't have. He had the anointing of the pastor or shepherd. I didn't have that anointing. That wasn't my call.

I tell you, a lot of people don't fit correctly where they are because they're in the wrong office. They're trying to fill the wrong office, and they don't have the anointing to do it. It's sort of like trying to put a square peg in a round hole. It just doesn't work.

THE PURPOSE OF THE ANOINTING: TO SET PEOPLE FREE

There is an anointing that goes with each of the five ministry offices. And we know that the Lord Jesus was anointed to stand in all five offices because He was anointed without measure. We read in our text in Luke 4:18 and 19 about what Jesus was anointed to do. It says He was anointed to preach, but He was also anointed to heal.

It also says in Acts 10:38, *"How God ANOINTED Jesus of Nazareth with the Holy Ghost and with power: who went about doing good, and HEALING all that were oppressed of the devil; for God was with him."* So we see in this verse the *healing* anointing.

We read from our text in Isaiah 10:27 that it's the anointing that destroys or breaks the yoke. Well, since Jesus was anointed with the Holy Ghost and power to *heal*, then that scripture in Isaiah could be talking about the yoke of sickness. Sickness is like a yoke upon a person; it holds him in bondage.

Notice Jesus said in Luke 4:18, "He has sent Me to preach deliverance to the *captives*." That has more than one meaning.

You see, some people are *spiritual* captives. But if you've ever been sick, you know that people can be *physical* captives too; they're captive to sickness and disease. But, thank God, there *is* deliverance!

THE MINISTRY OF JESUS

Jesus' ministry was not just limited to healing. We know that because He said in John 14:12, *"Verily, verily, I say unto you, He that believeth on me, the WORKS [plural] that I do shall he do also; and greater works than these shall he do; because I go unto my Father."* So His ministry was not just limited to healing, but for the purpose of this book, I'm singling out healing.

To do the works of Jesus—the same works that Jesus did—we'll have to have the same means that Jesus had to do those works. In other words, we'll have to use the same methods. So it is of utmost importance that we study the Word of God and learn something about the operation of the Spirit of God.

Why? Because we're not going to heal people with any power that *we* have of ourselves or by our own ability individually or physically. We're not going to be able to accomplish these things from the natural standpoint. But, thank God, the Holy Spirit *through* us *can* accomplish those things!

ZECHARIAH 4:6

6 Then he answered and spake unto me, saying, This is the word of the Lord unto Zerubbabel, saying, Not by might, nor by power, but by my spirit, saith the Lord of hosts.

Now we usually think of "might" and "power" in connection with the Spirit of God. We read in Acts 10:38, *"How God anointed Jesus of Nazareth with the Holy Ghost and with POWER: who went about doing good, and healing all that were oppressed of the devil; for God was with him."* The words "power" and "anointed" or "anointing" here are synonymous terms.

Zechariah 4:6 said, *"Not by might, nor by power . . . ,"* but here, "might" and "power" don't refer to the Spirit of God. The margin of my Bible says, "not by *army*" instead of "not by *might.*"

In other words, this verse is saying, "Not by *army*, nor by power . . . ." That means it's not by the might or power of an army that victory comes, but it's by the Spirit of God!

Then we read another Old Testament verse concerning the anointing or the Spirit of God: *"The yoke shall be destroyed because of the ANOINTING"* (Isa. 10:27).

The yoke of sickness, disease, or any bondage shall be destroyed because of the anointing! Or sometimes we say it like this: "It's the anointing that breaks the yoke!"

Now in this book, we're talking about the healing anointing and how it breaks the yoke of sickness. And as I mentioned earlier, in order to do justice to an intelligent study of the healing anointing, we need to talk about the ministry of Jesus.

We need to understand how the anointing works. For example, what makes the anointing work? Does it always work? What will keep the anointing from working? We will answer all of these questions in this book by studying very carefully the ministry of the Lord Jesus Christ, because He ministered under the anointing.

LUKE 4:18-19

18 The Spirit of the Lord is upon me [Jesus], because he hath anointed me to preach the gospel to the poor; he hath sent me to heal the brokenhearted, to preach deliverance to the captives,

and recovering of sight to the blind, to set at liberty them that are
bruised,

19 To preach the acceptable year of the Lord.

Jesus said, "The Spirit of the Lord is upon Me because He's
anointed Me." The Lord anointed Jesus primarily to do two things
according to this verse: to *preach* and to *heal.*

And we understand, of course, that in connection with preaching,
Jesus was also anointed to *teach.* So we could say it this way: "The
Lord anointed Jesus to *speak*—to preach and teach—and to *heal.*"

Of course, if you talk about the ministry of the Lord Jesus
Christ, many people will immediately say, "Yes, but Jesus was the
Son of God. That's why *He* was anointed."

But what those people fail to realize is that Jesus the Person is
one side of the coin, so to speak, and Jesus the Minister is another
side altogether.

JESUS HAD TO BE ANOINTED TO MINISTER

Of course, Jesus was and is the Son of God. But Jesus was not
ministering as the Son of God. He was *ministering* as a mere man
anointed by the Holy Ghost! If Jesus was ministering on the earth
as the Son of God and not as a man, then He wouldn't need to be
anointed. But the Bible plainly says Jesus was anointed to minister
on the earth.

LUKE 4:18

18 The Spirit of the Lord is upon me, because HE HATH
ANOINTED ME to preach the gospel to the poor; he hath sent me

to heal the brokenhearted, to preach deliverance to the captives, and recovering of sight to the blind, to set at liberty them that are bruised.

ACTS 10:38
38 How GOD ANOINTED JESUS of Nazareth with the Holy Ghost and with power: who went about doing good, and healing all that were oppressed of the devil; for God was with him.

If you didn't do any in-depth studying of the Bible at all, you could still see from these verses that Jesus was anointed by God to minister. He didn't minister as the Son of God; He ministered as a man anointed by God. In other words, Jesus had to be *anointed* to minister.

If you just thought about it a little bit, you'd know that. That's our problem many times: we don't have enough thinkers. Many folks just follow along with whatever has been said or whatever their church tradition says instead of stopping to think a little bit.

In Luke 4:18, Jesus said as He read from the Book of Isaiah, *"The Spirit of the Lord is upon me, because he hath anointed me to preach the gospel to the poor; he hath sent me TO HEAL . . . ."*

After Jesus finished reading, He closed the Book, handed it back to the minister, and sat down and taught the people. Jesus said, "This day is this scripture fulfilled in your hearing."

We can see certain truths from this passage of scripture in Luke chapter 4. One thing we can see is that if Jesus was ministering just as the Son of God—as God manifested in the flesh—He wouldn't need to be anointed. If Jesus was ministering as God manifested in the flesh, would God need to be anointed? I mean, who's going to anoint *God*!

Philippians chapter 2 sheds some more light on this.

PHILIPPIANS 2:6–8

6 Who [Jesus], being in the form of God, thought it not robbery to be equal with God:

7 BUT MADE HIMSELF OF NO REPUTATION, and TOOK UPON HIM THE FORM OF A SERVANT, and WAS MADE IN THE LIKENESS OF MEN:

8 And BEING FOUND IN FASHION AS A MAN, he humbled himself, and became obedient unto death, even the death of the cross.

Verse 7 is a little bit blind to us in the *King James Version*: *"But made himself of no reputation, and took upon him the form of a servant, and was made in the likeness of men."*

We don't get the full import of that: "He made Himself of no reputation." One other translation said He stripped Himself of His mighty power and glory when He came into this world, and He became as men.

Even though He was the Son of God, He became as a man. In other words, Jesus laid aside His mighty power and glory when He came to the earth. How did He do it? I don't know. The Bible plainly said He did it, so I just believe it.

That's the reason we do not see Jesus ministering as the Son of God in His earthly ministry. For example, Jesus was just as much the Son of God when He was *twenty-one* years old as He was at the time He was *thirty* years old when He was specially anointed by God. Yet the Bible never mentions that He healed anybody or wrought any miracles prior to the time He was specially anointed by God to do so (Luke 3:22; John 2:11).

Jesus was just as much the Son of God when He was *twenty-five* years old as He was when He was thirty. Yet even at age twenty-five, He had not worked miracles or healed anybody.

Jesus was just as much the Son of God all those years before He was anointed by God. Yet in all those years, He never healed one single person or wrought one single miracle until He was anointed by God. How do we know that? Because the Bible said so!

MARK 1:9–11

9   And it came to pass in those days, that Jesus came from Nazareth of Galilee, and was baptized of John in Jordan.

10 And straightway coming up out of the water, he saw the heavens opened, and THE SPIRIT LIKE A DOVE DESCENDING UPON HIM.

11 And there came a voice from heaven, saying, Thou art my beloved Son, in whom I am well pleased.

That's when Jesus was anointed to heal and work miracles— when the Spirit like a dove descended upon Him.

Then after that, the Word of God tells us about Jesus' returning to Cana of Galilee and attending the wedding feast with His mother. That's when He turned the water into wine. And the Bible said, *"This BEGINNING of miracles did Jesus in Cana of Galilee, and manifested forth his glory; and his disciples believed on him"* (John 2:11).

So, you see, Jesus had to be anointed before He could heal or work miracles. The reason for that was that Jesus had laid aside His mighty power and glory as the Son of God (Phil. 2:7–8). In *Person*, Jesus was the Son of God. But in *power*, He ministered as a man. He did not minister just as the Son of God. He had to be *anointed* to minister.

Yet you still hear some people say, "Well, certainly people received healing under Jesus' ministry—Jesus was the Son of God. That's why people were healed."

But when folks say that, they are really saying that no one else could ever minister and get people healed. They are saying that only Jesus could get people healed because He was the Son of God. But that simply isn't true.

WE SHOULD DO THE WORKS OF JESUS

Concerning ministry, those folks are putting Jesus in a class by Himself. Now in Person, He *is* in a class by Himself because Jesus is the Son of God. But in ministry, He is *not* in a class by Himself. Why? Because in John 14:12, Jesus said, *"He that believeth on me, the works that I do SHALL HE DO ALSO; and greater works than these shall he do; because I go unto my Father."*

If Jesus' works were in a class by themselves, then Jesus Himself told a falsehood, because He said, *". . . the works that I do shall he do also; and greater works than these shall he do."* So Jesus did not place His works or His ministry in a class by itself.

We have not really thoroughly studied the Word on the subject of the anointing. We have been religiously brainwashed, and we've thought, "Jesus was the Son of God. That's why He could minister healing. Therefore, I couldn't minister healing."

And, of course, when we've thought that, we've missed it in our thinking and our believing. So then, let's examine carefully the anointing in the ministry of Jesus and how the anointing works today. Then we can begin to understand how to tap into the healing power, and many will be blessed and helped.

LUKE 4:18

18 The Spirit of the Lord is upon me, because he HATH ANOINTED me to preach the gospel to the poor; he hath sent me TO HEAL the brokenhearted, to preach deliverance to the captives, and recovering of sight to the blind, to set at liberty them that are bruised.

ACTS 10:38

38 How GOD ANOINTED JESUS OF NAZARETH with the Holy Ghost and with power: who went about doing good, and HEAL-ING all that were oppressed of the devil; for God was with him.

Many times we have read these verses and then formed our own opinion of how we thought the anointing ought to work. But the only way in the world to find out how this healing anointing operates and how it is activated is just simply to go to the four Gospels and see what happened concerning the healing anointing in Jesus' ministry.

Let's look at another passage of scripture that describes the anointing under the ministry of Jesus.

MARK 5:25–30

25 And a certain woman, which had an issue of blood twelve years,

26 And had suffered many things of many physicians, and had spent all that she had, and was nothing bettered, but rather grew worse,

27 When she had heard of Jesus, came in the press behind, and touched his garment.

28 For she said, If I may touch but his clothes, I shall be whole.

29 And straightway the fountain of her blood was dried up; and she felt in her body that she was healed of that plague.

30 And Jesus, immediately knowing in himself that VIRTUE [or power—the anointing] had gone out of him, turned him about in the press, and said, Who touched my clothes?

That word "virtue" in verse 30 is a little misleading. Jesus wasn't anointed with *virtue*; He was anointed with *power*. In most reference Bibles, you'll notice either a small letter or number by the word "virtue." And the margin note references *power* or *dunamis*. In other words, here and throughout the New Testament, "dunamis" is the Greek word that is also translated *power*. "Dunamis" is the same word from which we get our English word "dynamite."

You could read other scriptures and know that virtue in Mark 5:30 is talking about power or the anointing. We already read one of those scriptures: *"The SPIRIT OF THE LORD is upon me, because he hath ANOINTED me"* (Luke 4:18).

—14—

You remember Peter said in Acts 10:38, *"How God ANOINTED Jesus of Nazareth with the HOLY GHOST and with POWER: who went about doing good, and HEALING."*

Notice the word "power" in that verse. Then notice in Mark 5:30 it says Jesus knew immediately that *virtue* or *power* had gone out of Him. What was that power? It was the power with which Jesus was *anointed*, not power that was His because He was the Son of God.

MARK 5:30

30 And Jesus, immediately knowing in himself that virtue [power] had gone out of him, turned him about in the press, and said, Who touched my clothes?

God anointed Jesus with that power to minister. What did Jesus minister? Well, for one, we know He ministered *healing.*

Now let's look at Matthew 14 and see another instance that illustrates the healing anointing.

MATTHEW 14:34-36

34 And when they were gone over, they came into the land of Gennesaret.

35 And when the men of that place had knowledge of him [Jesus], they sent out into all that country round about, and brought unto him all that were diseased;

36 And besought him that they might only TOUCH THE HEM OF HIS GARMENT: and as many as touched WERE MADE PERFECTLY WHOLE.

Although the healing anointing isn't specifically mentioned in this passage of scripture, it does imply that the diseased were healed in the same way the woman with the issue of blood was healed in Mark 5—by touching Jesus' clothes.

Mark 5:30 says that virtue or power went out of Jesus when the woman with the issue of blood touched His clothes. So we can conclude that the diseased in the land of Gennesaret in Matthew 14:36 were also healed by the healing power or anointing when they touched the hem of Jesus' garment.

THE ANOINTING MAKES THE DIFFERENCE!

Mark chapter 5 states that healing power went out of Jesus when the woman with the issue of blood touched His clothes. You remember Jesus said, "Who touched My clothes?" (v. 30). What was so special about Jesus' clothes that the woman received healing? It was the anointing!

Now let's look at another instance of the healing anointing flowing out to the sick through cloth.

ACTS 19:11-12

11 And God wrought special miracles by the hands of Paul:

12 So that from his body were brought unto the sick handkerchiefs or aprons, and the DISEASES DEPARTED from them, and the EVIL SPIRITS WENT OUT OF THEM.

Although the words "anointing," "Holy Spirit," or "power" are not used in these verses, you know that the anointing—the Holy Spirit or the power of God—was in manifestation. Why? Because just an ordinary handkerchief, apron, or piece of cloth wouldn't cause evil spirits to leave people. If it did, then no one who wore clothes would have any demons! Yet we are conscious and aware that some people do have demons or evil spirits.

And if just a piece of cloth alone would cause sickness to leave people, we wouldn't have any disease among us, because everyone who had a handkerchief in his pocket or had on a shirt or a dress or any type of cloth would be healed.

But cloths don't heal people. Cloths don't cause demons to leave people. No, in Acts 19:11 and 12, there had to be something *special* about those handkerchiefs and aprons that caused diseases and evil spirits to depart from people. What was it? It was God! It was the anointing!

God performed special miracles by the hands of Paul. We can understand *how* He wrought special miracles by reading Acts 10:38 concerning the ministry of Jesus.

ACTS 10:38
38 How God ANOINTED Jesus of Nazareth with the HOLY GHOST and with POWER: who went about doing good, and healing all that were oppressed of the devil; for God was with him.

ACTS 19:11
11 And God WROUGHT SPECIAL MIRACLES by the hands of Paul.

God wrought special miracles through the hands of Paul by the same means Jesus used to heal "all that were oppressed of the devil"—by the *anointing*!

God is the subject of both Acts 10:38 and Acts 19:11. *God* anointed Jesus of Nazareth, and *God* wrought special miracles by the hands of Paul. We're talking about two different ministries—the ministry of Jesus and the ministry of Paul. But it was God who did the work in both ministries. God anointed the Lord Jesus Christ to heal, and He wrought miracles through the Apostle Paul.

Someone said, "Of course, *Jesus* was anointed to heal! Jesus was the Son of God!" But the Bible says that although Jesus was the Son of God, He laid aside all of His mighty power and glory and became a man (Phil. 2:6,7). And the Bible says God *anointed* Him.

Notice in Acts 19:11 that God wrought those special miracles by the *hands* of Paul through the anointing. Then it says, *"So that from his [Paul's] BODY were brought unto the sick handkerchiefs or aprons . . ."* (v. 12). Well, Paul's *hands* were a part of Paul's *body*, weren't they? Evidently, Paul handled or laid his hands upon those cloths, and the anointing that was upon Paul was transferred into the cloths and accomplished some marvelous results. The power that was in the cloths was transmitted to the bodies of the sick. When that power was transmitted, diseases and evil spirits departed!

You see, those people weren't healed by touching *Paul*—they were healed by touching the handkerchiefs or aprons that had touched his body. When Paul laid his hands on those handkerchiefs or cloths, the cloths absorbed the same anointing Paul was anointed with. Then the power went out of those cloths and healed people.

The same thing happened in Jesus' ministry when the sick touched His clothes. Jesus' clothes absorbed the same anointing

Jesus was anointed with. Then as the anointing came in contact with the sick, the sick were healed!

Therefore, we could rightly conclude that since the Bible said that God wrought special miracles by the hands of Paul, He anointed Paul in a similar manner as He anointed Jesus.

We could also conclude this: Jesus' clothes and the handkerchiefs of Paul became saturated with this power or anointing!

Notice in some of the cases of healing under Jesus' ministry that we've covered, the sick didn't actually touch Jesus. They touched *the hem of His garment* or *His clothes,* and they were made perfectly whole because of the *anointing.* The anointing is transferable, and we will look at this characteristic of the anointing again later. But right now I want you to see that the sick in Matthew 14:36 were healed by the anointing. And who anointed Jesus? God did!

MATTHEW 14:36

36 And [they] besought him [Jesus] that they might only TOUCH THE HEM OF HIS GARMENT: and as many as touched WERE MADE PERFECTLY WHOLE.

Also, did you ever stop and think about the fact that even Jesus never claimed to do any miracles Himself or in His own power? He said, "The Father in Me, *He* doeth the works."

JOHN 14:10

10 Believest thou not that I am in the Father, and the Father in me? the words that I speak unto you I speak NOT OF MYSELF: but the Father that dwelleth in me, HE doeth the works.

In other words, Jesus was saying, "*I* don't do the works. It's the Father who dwells in Me—*He* does the works." And the Bible tells us in Acts 10:38 how the Father did the works: *"God ANOINTED Jesus of Nazareth with the HOLY GHOST and with POWER."*

That's how the Father did the works—by the anointing! So whether it was the clothes of Jesus or the handkerchiefs of Paul, it was the anointing that made the difference!

CHARACTERISTICS OF THE ANOINTING

We've already briefly looked at the similarities between Acts 10:38 and Acts 19:11 and 12. Let's look further at another similarity.

ACTS 10:38

38 How GOD ANOINTED Jesus of Nazareth with the Holy Ghost and with power: who went about doing good, and healing all that were oppressed of the devil; for God was with him.

ACTS 19:11-12

11 And GOD WROUGHT special miracles by the hands of Paul:

12 So that from his body were brought unto the sick handkerchiefs or aprons, and the diseases departed from them, and the evil spirits went out of them.

In analyzing these two verses, we notice that one verse begins *"How GOD ANOINTED . . . ,"* and the other verse begins *"And GOD WROUGHT . . . ."*

God *anointed* and God *wrought*! But notice who did the "doing" in both verses—*God*!

That's not the only similarity between those two verses. We can see another similarity between the handkerchiefs or aprons brought from Paul's body, and the garments of Jesus. In both cases, the anointing was transmitted through *cloth*.

MATTHEW 14:35–36

35 And when the men of that place had knowledge of him [Jesus], they sent out into all that country round about, and brought unto him all that were diseased;

36 And besought him that they might only touch the HEM OF HIS GARMENT: and as many as touched were made perfectly whole.

You'll notice in Matthew chapter 14, that those people sought to touch the hem of Jesus' garment. They didn't touch *Him*; they just touched the hem of His *garment*, and they were healed!

Then in Mark's Gospel, we read that the woman with the issue of blood *"came in the press behind, and touched his* [Jesus'] *garment"* (Mark 5:27). Well, evidently, Jesus' garment became charged with that same power or anointing that He Himself was anointed with.

Also, the cloths that Paul laid hands upon (Acts 19:11–12) became charged with the same anointing that Paul was anointed with, which was the healing and delivering power of God.

Then it seems that the healing power of God can be absorbed by certain materials, namely cloths. And that healing power or anointing can be transmitted or transferred into the bodies of the sick.

THE ANOINTING IS TRANSMITTABLE

So we know that the anointing is *transmittable*. Now let's look further at *how* the anointing is transmitted. The anointing with which God anointed Jesus was absorbed into Jesus' clothing. We read that the multitude of people in Gennesaret just sought to touch the hem of His garment—not *Jesus*—but His *garment.*

And it says that as many as touched Him were made perfectly whole (Matt. 14:36). So we know that Jesus' garment as well as Jesus Himself must have been full of that power. His garment had absorbed the power that was upon Him. So we know that there's something about this power that can be absorbed into and transmitted through certain materials.

LAWS THAT GOVERN THE ANOINTING

We read in Acts 19:12 that from Paul's body "were brought unto the sick handkerchiefs or aprons." Well, why didn't the people bring rocks instead of cloths? Why did they bring cloths? They could have gotten some little pebbles and brought them to Paul to be anointed!

Rev. John G. Lake made a very interesting statement along this line. John Lake was mightily anointed of God and used tremendously by the Spirit of God. Rev. Lake said that *electricity* is God's power in the *natural* realm, and *Holy Ghost power* is God's power in the *spiritual* realm.

In other words, in the natural realm, electricity is a power. But not every kind of metal conducts electricity. Only certain kinds of metals conduct it. There are certain laws that govern the operation of electricity — it is transmitted from one place to another under certain conditions. Under wrong conditions, electricity will not be conducted or transmitted.

In much the same way, in the spiritual realm, there is this mighty power of God—the anointing. Yet evidently, not every kind of substance conducts it either. But apparently, cloth will act as a conductor of the power of God, because we read that Jesus' garment absorbed the power to the extent that all who touched even the hem of His clothes were made well.

You'd have to come to the conclusion from reading the scripture that the healing power of God is transmittable just as electricity is transmittable and that the anointing is governed by certain laws just as electricity in the natural is governed by certain laws.

In other words, there are certain conditions under which the power of God can be transmitted, because only certain materials can absorb and conduct God's power. The opposite is also true. There are certain materials that *cannot* absorb and conduct the healing power (we'll talk more about that later).

The handkerchiefs and aprons in Acts 19:11 and 12 that were brought from the body of Paul unto the sick evidently *did* absorb that power. God's power flowed out of Paul into those cloths and saturated them with the anointing. Then as the cloths were laid on the sick, that power was then transmitted or transferred into their bodies. The anointing or power surcharged their bodies, and the diseases departed and the evil spirits went out of them (v. 12).

Modernists have said that the biblical account of specially anointed cloths being brought to the sick was just a superstition. But it's not; it's Bible *fact*. It happened just exactly like the Bible said it happened.

The Bible is God's infallible Word. Through the Psalmist, God said concerning His Word, *"For ever, O Lord, thy word is settled in heaven"* (Ps. 119:89). And since God's Word said it, I believe it, and that settles it! Hallelujah!

THE MANTLE OF GOD'S ANOINTING

There is another very interesting incident in the scripture that has to do with the power of God and the laws that govern the transmission of that power.

1 KINGS 19:16, 19

16 And Jehu the son of Nimshi shalt thou [Elijah] ANOINT to be KING over Israel: and ELISHA the son of Shaphat of Abelmeholah shalt thou ANOINT to be PROPHET in thy room [or in thy stead or place] . . . .

19 So he departed thence, and found Elisha the son of Shaphat, who was plowing with twelve yoke of oxen before him, and he with the twelfth: and Elijah passed by him, and CAST HIS MANTLE UPON HIM.

There was an anointing to stand in the office of prophet, and there was an anointing to stand in other offices or positions such as that of a king.

Elijah would anoint with oil those whom God appointed as king or prophet. But, you see, that oil is a type of the Holy Spirit. And when God told Elijah to anoint someone with oil, that meant the Holy Ghost was going to come upon that person to anoint and enable him to be king or to stand in a particular office.

Elijah's casting his mantle upon Elisha in verse 19 signified that the Holy Ghost was going to come upon Elisha to anoint him to be prophet in the place of Elijah.

After Elijah cast his mantle upon Elisha, Elisha began to follow Elijah.

2 KINGS 2:1–8

1 And it came to pass, when the Lord would take up Elijah into heaven by a whirlwind, that Elijah went with Elisha from Gilgal.

2 And Elijah said unto Elisha, Tarry [or wait] here, I pray thee; for the Lord hath sent me to Beth-el. And Elisha said unto him, As the Lord liveth, and as thy soul liveth, I will not leave thee. So they went down to Bethel.

3 And the sons of the prophets that were at Bethel came forth to Elisha, and said unto him, Knowest thou that the Lord will take away thy master from thy head to day? And he said, Yea, I know it; hold ye your peace.

4 And Elijah said unto him, Elisha, tarry here, I pray thee; for the Lord hath sent me to Jericho. And he said, As the Lord liveth, and as thy soul liveth, I will not leave thee. So they came to Jericho.

5 And the sons of the prophets that were at Jericho came to Elisha, and said unto him, Knowest thou that the Lord will take away thy master from thy head to day? And he answered, Yea, I know it; hold ye your peace.

6 And Elijah said unto him, Tarry, I pray thee, here; for the Lord hath sent me to Jordan. And he said, As the Lord liveth, and as thy soul liveth, I will not leave thee. And they two went on.

7 And fifty men of the sons of the prophets went, and stood to view afar off: and they two stood by Jordan.

8 And Elijah took his MANTLE, and wrapped [or folded] it together, and SMOTE THE WATERS, and they WERE DIVIDED HITHER AND THITHER, so that THEY TWO WENT OVER ON DRY GROUND.

We'll not go into an in-depth study here, but in the past, I have done an in-depth study on the mantle. Very often in the Old Testament, the word "mantle" meant *a loose outer garment.*

Did you notice verse 8 said Elijah took his mantle, *folded it together,* and smote the waters? In other words, the mantle was just an outer garment. Sometimes it was just like a loose-fitting topcoat you'd wear over everything else you had on. That's the reason Elijah could throw the mantle over Elijah (1 Kings 19:19); it was a loose outer garment.

In my own personal experience, many times as I've ministered, I've been conscious of the fact that suddenly I could feel a mantle or an anointing come down upon me. It was just as if someone threw a coat over my shoulders. I could feel it all over me.

For example, if someone came along behind me and threw a topcoat over my shoulders, don't you think I could feel that? Well, in ministering under the anointing many times, that's the way it feels to me. I feel that mantle over my entire being.

That's scriptural. It's a scriptural manifestation. And when the anointing comes upon a person like that, some very interesting things can happen that will bless people.

Let's look at Second Kings 2:8 concerning the mantle or cloak of Elijah, where we can see another example of the transmission of the anointing into cloth.

2 KINGS 2:8

8   And Elijah took his mantle [outer garment or cloak], and wrapped it together, and smote the waters, and they were divided hither and thither . . . .

Now again, it wasn't the cloak that divided the waters, just like it wasn't the clothes of Jesus or the handkerchiefs of Paul that healed people. Remember we said that just ordinary cloth couldn't heal anybody. If it could, then no one who wore clothes would ever be sick. It was the anointing that flowed through the clothes of Jesus and the handkerchiefs of Paul that made the difference.

Well, other people besides Elijah had outer garments or mantles. But Elijah's cloak stood for something; it represented the supernatural. Evidently, it absorbed the anointing with which Elijah was anointed. So when Elijah smote the waters, they were divided "hither and thither" so that Elijah and Elisha went over on dry ground.

THE ANOINTING IS MEASURABLE

We see another characteristic of the anointing in connection with Elijah and Elisha. Not only is the anointing transmittable or transferable, it is also measurable.

2 KINGS 2:9

9 And it came to pass, when they were gone over, that Elijah said unto Elisha, Ask what I shall do for thee, before I be taken away from thee. And Elisha said, I pray thee, LET A DOUBLE PORTION OF THY SPIRIT [the Spirit that was upon Elijah] be upon me.

Elisha asked for a double portion of Elijah's anointing, and from reading the scriptures, apparently God gave it to him.

2 KINGS 2:10‒15

10 And he [Elijah] said [to Elisha], Thou hast asked a hard thing: nevertheless, if thou see me when I am taken from thee, it shall be so unto thee; but if not, it shall not be so.

11 And it came to pass, as they still went on, and talked, that, behold, there appeared a chariot of fire, and horses of fire, and parted them both asunder; and Elijah went up by a whirlwind into heaven.

12 And Elisha saw it, and he cried, My father, my father, the chariot of Israel, and the horsemen thereof. And he saw him no more: and HE TOOK HOLD OF HIS OWN CLOTHES, and RENT THEM IN TWO PIECES.

13 He TOOK UP ALSO THE MANTLE OF ELIJAH that fell from him, and went back, and stood by the bank of Jordan;

14 And he TOOK THE MANTLE OF ELIJAH that fell from him, and SMOTE THE WATERS, and said, Where is the Lord God of Elijah? and when he also had smitten the waters, THEY PARTED HITHER AND THITHER: and Elisha went over.

15 And when the sons of the prophets which were to view at Jericho saw him, they said, THE SPIRIT OF ELIJAH DOTH REST ON ELISHA. And they came to meet him, and bowed themselves to the ground before him.

Elisha asked for a double portion of the same anointing with which Elijah was anointed. Elijah said to Elisha, *"Thou hast asked a hard thing: nevertheless, if thou see me when I am taken from thee, it shall be so unto thee; but if not, it shall not be so"* (v. 10).

Well, verse 12 says Elisha did see Elijah being taken up "by a whirlwind into Heaven," so apparently, Elisha received a double portion of the anointing that was upon Elijah.

THE ANOINTING IN A DEAD MAN'S BONES

Elisha became the prophet in Israel in Elijah's place or stead. We can read in Second Kings chapters 2–13 about the miracles that were performed as a result of the double portion of Elijah's anointing that came upon Elisha.

But now go to Second Kings 13:20, and let's look at one effect of the double portion of the anointing that Elisha had even after he died and was buried.

2 KINGS 13:20–21

20 And Elisha died, and they buried him. And the bands of the Moabites invaded the land at the coming in of the year.

21 And it came to pass, as they were burying a man, that, behold, they spied a band of men; and they cast the man into the sepulchre of Elisha: and when THE MAN WAS LET DOWN, and TOUCHED THE BONES OF ELISHA, he REVIVED, and STOOD UP ON HIS FEET.

The anointing that was upon Elisha even after he died was powerful enough to raise from the dead a man who came in contact with Elisha's bones!

Glory to God! Now how do you suppose that happened to this man? There was a residue of *anointing*—of the power of God—left in the bones of Elisha! Even after the flesh had rotted off Elisha's bones, there was enough anointing arrayed in those bones to raise a man from the dead!

Now *Elijah* had a *portion* of the Spirit. He'd had an anointing upon him to stand in the office of prophet. And Elijah didn't die. The Bible says he went up into Heaven by a whirlwind, a chariot of fire, and so forth. But *Elisha* had a *double portion* of the anointing Elijah had and yet Elisha died. He wasn't received up into Heaven by a whirlwind.

I don't know why that is. I don't know everything, and I'm not "running the show," are you? No, of course you're not. *God* is running the show. So let's just trust Him.

Someone said, "Well, why didn't the anointing raise *Elisha* from the dead?"

Well, you never read in the Bible where an old person was raised from the dead. It was always either a baby, a young person, or a middle-aged person.

You see, God didn't say you were never going to die. He said, *"I will take sickness away from the midst of thee . . . [and] the NUMBER OF THY DAYS I WILL FULFIL"* (Exod. 23:25–26). Elisha had fulfilled his days. This other man who was thrown into Elisha's grave hadn't fulfilled his days. It's as simple as that.

It's interesting that the man wasn't raised from the dead until he came in contact with Elisha's bones. There had to be a connection between Elisha's bones and the man's being raised up, because it says when the man touched Elisha's *bones*, he was revived.

So there had to be something about Elisha's bones that caused that to happen, because just any bones wouldn't raise a person from the dead. Well, there *was* something about those bones that revived him. It was the anointing! Elisha's bones had absorbed the power with which he was anointed when he was alive.

In the same way, there was something in the garment of Jesus that caused the sick to be healed and devils to go. And there was something in those cloths that came from the body of Paul that caused demons and devils to leave people and diseases to depart from them. What was it? It was the anointing!

THE ANOINTING IS TANGIBLE

We learned that the anointing is *measurable*. We read in the Old Testament that God commanded the prophet Elijah to anoint Elisha to take his place, and it says Elisha asked for a *double portion* of Elijah's anointing (2 Kings 2:9).

Then in the Gospels we saw that Jesus was anointed to minister as He walked upon the earth. And it says in John 3:34 that Jesus had the anointing *without measure*. (We as individual members in the Body of Christ have the anointing *in a measure*.)

We also learned that the anointing is *transmittable*. In Mark 5, it says that Jesus knew immediately when virtue or power—the healing anointing—had gone out of Him (v. 30). And when it went out of Him, it passed through His clothes and went into the woman with the issue of blood. So the healing power of God is *transmittable* or *transferable*. Therefore, we also know that the healing power of God must be *tangible*.

Now the word "tangible" means *perceptible to the touch*. In other words, something that is tangible is capable of being touched.

For example, we know that the anointing that went into the woman with the issue of blood was tangible because Jesus knew *immediately* when that power went out of Him. Jesus was aware of an *outflow* of that healing power, and the woman was aware of the *reception* of that power. So the power had to have been tangible.

The tangible healing anointing is the power of God to heal and to undo the work of the enemy in a person's life. And that anointing works, or is transmitted and effects a healing and a cure, in connection with the person believing in it, as I'll discuss later.

Well, if you can believe that the bones of a *dead* prophet could revive the dead (and you can, because it's Bible), then it ought to be comparatively easy to believe that the hands of a *living* prophet could minister healing to you.

It ought to be an easy, simple thing to believe that a minister today could be anointed to minister the healing anointing to you.

You can believe it because the Lord never changes, and the healing anointing is available to you today!

We've just never learned as we should have about the anointing or power of God. We knew it was there, but maybe we've been afraid to explore it or thought we *shouldn't* explore it. But, thank God, that's changing, and we are studying and learning more and more about the anointing.

There is a lot we need to learn yet about the anointing. I don't know about you, but I don't know everything! However, I'm so glad I know more today than I did yesterday! And I'm going to know more tomorrow. I'm going to know more next week, next month, and next year about the anointing and the healing power of God!

---

[1]For a further study on the different types of anointings, *see* Rev. Hagin's book *Understanding the Anointing.*

—Chapter 2—

RECEIVING HEALING
THROUGH THE ANOINTING

And a certain woman, which had an issue of blood twelve years,

And had suffered many things of many physicians, and had spent all that she had, and was nothing bettered, but rather grew worse,

When she had heard of Jesus, came in the press behind, and touched his garment.

For she said, If I may touch but his clothes, I shall be whole.

And straightway the fountain of her blood was dried up; and she felt in her body that she was healed of that plague.

And Jesus, immediately knowing in himself that virtue [power] had gone out of him, turned him about in the press, and said, Who touched my clothes?

And his disciples said unto him, Thou seest the multitude thronging thee, and sayest thou, Who touched me?

And he looked round about to see her that had done this thing.

But the woman fearing and trembling, knowing what was done in her, came and fell down before him, and told him all the truth.

And he said unto her, Daughter, THY FAITH hath made thee whole; go in peace, and be whole of thy plague.

—Mark 5:25–34

And when they were gone over, they came into the land of Gennesaret.

And when the men of that place had knowledge of him [Jesus], they sent out into all that country round about, and brought unto him all that were diseased;

And besought him that they might only touch the hem of his garment: and as many as touched were made perfectly whole.

—Matthew 14:34–36

This passage in Matthew 14 doesn't mention the word "power" or "anointing" as such, but we know exactly what happened from reading Mark 5:30 and other scriptures. The people who touched Jesus' garment were healed by their faith in the healing anointing or power with which Jesus was anointed.

LUKE 6:17-19

17   And he came down with them, and stood in the plain, and the company of his disciples, and a great multitude of people out of all Judaea and Jerusalem, and from the sea coast of Tyre and Sidon, which came TO HEAR HIM, and TO BE HEALED of their diseases;

18   And they that were vexed with unclean spirits: and they were healed.

19   And the whole multitude sought to touch him: for there went VIRTUE [power] OUT OF HIM, and HEALED THEM all.

In all three cases—in Mark chapter 5, Matthew chapter 14, and Luke chapter 6, the people involved were healed through Jesus' ministry by the healing anointing. The healing anointing or power of God was activated on their behalf and brought healing to their bodies *through their faith*!

How do I know that? Well, in Mark chapter 5, Jesus plainly told the woman with the issue of blood, *"Daughter, THY FAITH hath made thee whole; go in peace, and be whole of thy plague"* (v. 34). Then Matthew 14 states that when the people had knowledge of Jesus, they brought the sick unto Him and He healed them. Well, how did they have knowledge of Jesus? By *hearing* something about Him.

And we know that *"FAITH cometh by HEARING, and HEARING by the word of God"* (Rom. 10:17). The Bible says in Mark 5:27, *"When she had HEARD of Jesus, came in the press behind, and touched his garment."* Jesus plainly said this woman had faith and that it was her faith that made her whole (v. 34). Well, how did the woman get faith. She *heard* about Jesus. What did she hear? She must have heard that Jesus was anointed!

The same thing is inferred in Luke 6:17–19 concerning the multitude. Verse 17 says, *"a great multitude of people out of all Judaea and Jerusalem, and from the sea coast of Tyre and Sidon . . . came TO HEAR Him [Jesus], and TO BE HEALED of their diseases."*

THE HEARING COMES BEFORE THE HEALING

Notice they *heard* before they were healed. Since we know that faith comes by hearing, we could infer that since the multitude came to hear and be healed, faith came when they heard, and their faith made them whole too!

Then in Luke 6:17 it said, ". . . *a great multitude of people out of all Judaea and Jerusalem, and from the sea coast of Tyre and Sidon, which came TO HEAR him, and TO BE HEALED of their diseases.*" So in all three of these cases, the people were healed because they *heard* something. They heard that Jesus was anointed, and their faith mixed with the healing power brought healing to their bodies.

I want to emphasize again the fact that the folks in Luke 6 came, not just to be healed, but to *hear* and be healed. You see, that's where a lot of folks miss it. They want to be healed, but they don't want to hear. Very seldom do people get healed who will not hear.

In all of these cases in Mark 5, Matthew 14, and Luke 6, the *knowledge of Jesus* came first before the healing.

You see, you gain knowledge by hearing. When the woman with the issue of blood "had heard of Jesus," she gained knowledge of Him and went to Him to be healed (Mark 5:27). In Matthew 14 when the people gained knowledge of Him, they brought the sick to Him to be healed, and they were healed (vv. 35–36)! How did they gain knowledge of Jesus? The same way the woman with the issue of blood gained knowledge of Him! Someone *told* her about Jesus. What did someone tell her? That Jesus was *anointed!*

In the first vision I had when Jesus appeared to me (it was in Rockwall, Texas, on the second day of September back in 1950),

He told me to look in Luke chapter 4 where it says He went into the synagogue in Nazareth on the Sabbath day.

Jesus had not preached in the synagogue in Nazareth before that time. Nazareth was His hometown, and Jesus had just returned there after being baptized by the Holy Ghost. The Holy Ghost came upon Him in the Jordan and anointed Him. Then Jesus returned to Nazareth.

Jesus said to me when He appeared to me that day in 1950: "I read from the Book of Isaiah that the Spirit of the Lord was upon Me because He had anointed Me to do all those things among them" (Luke 4:18–20; Isa. 61:1–3).

Jesus continued: "Then when I finished reading, I closed the Book and taught the people." And Luke 4 says He sat down and taught the people, saying, "This day is this scripture fulfilled in your ears" (v. 21). In other words, Jesus said, "I'm anointed just as the scripture says I am."

Jesus told me, "I didn't preach that just in Nazareth. Everywhere I went, that was the first sermon I preached. Wherever I went, the first thing I did was tell people, 'This scripture is fulfilled in your ears. I'm anointed.'"

The people in the Gospels only had the Old Testament. They didn't have the New Testament (but we do, thank God). So everywhere Jesus went, He preached to people, taking His text from Isaiah.

ISAIAH 61:1–3

1   The SPIRIT OF THE LORD GOD is upon me; because the Lord
     hath ANOINTED me to preach good tidings unto the meek; he

hath sent me to bind up the brokenhearted, to proclaim liberty to the captives, and the opening of the prison to them that are bound;

2   To proclaim the acceptable year of the Lord, and the day of vengeance of our God; to comfort all that mourn;

3   To appoint unto them that mourn in Zion, to give unto them beauty for ashes, the oil of joy for mourning, the garment of praise for the spirit of heaviness; that they might be called trees of righteousness, the planting of the Lord, that he might be glorified.

Jesus said to me in the vision, "Those who believed what I told them would receive healing, and those who didn't believe it *didn't* receive healing."

We always imagine that everyone always received their needs met under Jesus' ministry, but they didn't. Why? Because some didn't believe or accept Him. For instance, the people didn't accept Jesus' ministry there in Nazareth (Luke 4:22–28), so they didn't receive healing.

In another place it says, *"And he could there* [in Nazareth] *do no mighty work, save that he laid his hands upon a few sick folk, and healed them"* (Mark 6:5).

Concerning Jesus' ministry in Nazareth, Mark 6:5 states that He only laid His hands upon a few sick people and healed them. Why did Jesus lay His hands upon only a few? Because when Jesus preached to the people in Nazareth, they wouldn't believe He was anointed to heal.

But in Matthew 14:36, we read that in Gennesaret, *"AS MANY AS TOUCHED* [the hem of Jesus' garment] *were made perfectly whole."*

MATTHEW 14:35-36

35 And when the men of that place [Gennesaret] HAD KNOWL-
EDGE OF HIM [Jesus] they sent out into all that country round
about, and brought unto him all that were diseased.

36 And besought him that they might only touch the hem of his garment: and AS MANY AS TOUCHED were made perfectly whole.

Look at the first part of verse 35, which says the men of Gennesaret had knowledge concerning Jesus. What do you suppose
was the knowledge they had of Him? Well, it must have been the
same knowledge that He'd shared with people elsewhere—that He
was anointed!

You'll remember that Mark chapter 5 says about the woman
with the issue of blood, *"When she had HEARD OF JESUS, came
in the press behind, and touched his garment."*

What did she hear of Jesus? I wonder what people told her
about Him? Well, they couldn't have told her that He died for her
sins, because He hadn't done that yet. No, they must have told
her what they had heard Him preach. What did they hear Him
preach? They heard Him say the same thing He said at Nazareth
in Luke 4:18: "I'm anointed." And the woman believed what she
heard.

YOU MUST BELIEVE WHAT
YOU HEAR FROM THE WORD

We can see then that it makes all the difference in the world as
to whether or not people believe what Jesus said.

—41—

LUKE 6:17-19

17 And he came down with them, and stood in the plain, and the company of his disciples, and a great multitude of people out of all Judaea and Jerusalem, and from the sea coast of Tyre and Sidon, which came to hear him, and to be healed of their diseases;

18 And they that were vexed with unclean spirits: and they were healed.

19 And the whole multitude sought to touch him: for there WENT VIRTUE OUT OF HIM, and HEALED THEM ALL.

Verse 19 is talking about the healing anointing—the healing *virtue* or the healing *power* of God. We can see a difference and a similarity between Mark chapter 5, which deals with the woman with the issue of blood, and this passage, Luke 6:17-19, which deals with the healing of the multitude. We can see that this anointing worked on an *individual* basis in one case and on a *collective* basis in the other case. But in both cases, it worked by *faith*. In other words, in both cases, the people heard about Jesus, and they believed and acted on what they heard.

Let's notice again Luke 6:17.

LUKE 6:17

17 And he came down with them, and stood in the plain, and the company of his disciples, and a great multitude of people out of all Judaea and Jerusalem, and from the sea coast of Tyre and Sidon, which came TO HEAR HIM, and TO BE HEALED OF THEIR DISEASES.

We know the woman with the issue of blood in Mark chapter 5 *heard* of Jesus. That's why she came to Him to be healed. And Luke 6:17 says the multitudes came to *hear* Him and to be healed of their diseases. Also, Matthew 14:35 states that the men of Genessaret *had knowledge* of Jesus and sent for the diseased to be brought unto Him. They gained knowledge of Jesus by *hearing* about Him.

Many times in the four Gospels, you'll read about a crowd or a multitude that came to Jesus and were healed, and it doesn't say by what method or how they were healed. It just says they were healed.

But Luke 6:17–19 goes into some detail about how they were healed. I think one of the reasons for that is that Luke, who wrote the book of Luke, was a doctor and was probably more interested than the other disciples in some of the details of the healings and miracles that occurred in Jesus' ministry.

Actually, Matthew, Mark, and Luke all recorded practically the same healings. For example, they all recorded the healing of the woman with the issue of blood. But John, the fourth writer of the Gospels, didn't. John did record a number of healings, but most of the healings he recorded—such as the nobleman's son in John chapter 4, the lame man at the pool of Bethesda in chapter 5, and the blind man in chapter 9—weren't recorded by the others.

It is interesting to note that in the case of Peter's mother-in-law who was sick with a fever, Matthew, Mark, and Luke all recorded the account. Yet both Matthew and Mark just said she was "sick of a fever" (Matt. 8:14; Mark 1:30). But Luke, being a physician, said she was *"taken with a GREAT fever"* (Luke 4:38).

If you've ever studied medical history, you'd know that at that particular time, people divided fever into two categories. They didn't know as much as medical science knows today, so they called a fever a *lesser* fever or a *greater* fever.

So Luke said certain things because he made more detailed observations than some of the others. He was more interested in that area. Now read what Luke has to say in Luke 6:19.

LUKE 6:19
19 And the whole multitude sought to touch him [why did the multitude seek to touch Him?]: FOR THERE WENT VIRTUE OUT OF HIM, and HEALED THEM ALL.

In other words, there went *power* or *anointing* out of Him and healed them all. Remember we read, *"How God anointed Jesus of Nazareth with THE HOLY GHOST and WITH POWER: who went about doing good, and HEALING all that were oppressed of the devil; for God was with him"* (Acts 10:38).

But notice in Luke 6:17 that those who were healed had to *hear* first!

LUKE 6:17
17 And he came down with them, and stood in the plain, and the company of his disciples, and a great multitude of people out of all Judaea and Jerusalem, and from the sea coast of Tyre and Sidon, which CAME TO HEAR HIM, and TO BE HEALED of their diseases.

They came to hear Jesus and to be healed. They didn't just come to be *healed*; they came to *hear* too.

BE CAREFUL HOW YOU HEAR

I found out that, usually, when you get people to hear, it's very simple to get them healed. But the biggest job is getting people to hear.

You see, many times people just *think* they're hearing, but they're not. I know that for a fact because I've heard people say, "Brother Hagin said such-and-such," and then they supposedly quoted me. But I never said any such thing. And I have told people, "I never said that."

"Well, what did you say then?" And when I told them what I actually said, they would reply, "Oh, I misunderstood you. I understood that you said such-and-such."

You know, it's amazing how people hear. No wonder Jesus said to take heed how you hear—not only *what* you hear, but *how* you hear (Luke 8:18).

HOW TO COOPERATE
WITH THE ANOINTING

We read about the woman in Mark 5 who was healed. Now her healing is a *fact*! But two things are mentioned in connection with her healing. There were ingredients mentioned that played a part in her receiving healing. We already talked about them briefly. What were they? *Faith* and *power*. She believed what she heard about Jesus—that He was anointed. And her faith in that healing power healed her and made her whole.

As we already read, electricity is God's power in the natural realm. But the Holy Ghost power is God's power in the supernatural realm! According to what the Bible tells us, we understand a lot about the supernatural, the unseen realm, by the *seen* realm (Rom. 1:20).

Well, electricity exists in the seen realm, and it is a power. It can be transmitted, yet just any and everything won't transmit that power. Only certain materials conduct or transmit the power of electricity.

The same is true with the "heavenly electricity"—the anointing or power of God. We know this much about it from the Word of God: Both the handkerchiefs and aprons that Paul laid hands on and the clothes that Jesus wore conducted that power. In other words, the healing power of God is transmittable or transferable.

Now we might ask the questions, "*How* is it transmittable? How does someone cooperate with the anointing!"

Well, how was the healing anointing transferred to the woman with the issue of blood? By her *faith*.

It says that Jesus knew immediately in Himself that power or anointing had gone out of Him (Mark 5:30). But He said in verse 34, *"Daughter, THY FAITH hath made thee whole."* Whose faith made her whole? It was *her* faith.

This woman with the issue of blood was healed by the healing anointing or power that flowed from Jesus' garment into the woman. But notice her faith had something to do with it.

We've discussed other instances in which the faith of the person seeking healing played a part in him or her receiving healing. For example, although faith is not directly mentioned, when Jesus passed with His disciples over the Sea of Galilee to the land of the Gennesaret, it says, *"When the men of that place HAD KNOWLEDGE OF HIM, they sent out into all that country round about, and brought unto him all that were diseased"* (Matt. 14:35).

You see, just because Jesus came to their vicinity and they saw Him, they didn't just automatically start gathering up the sick and the diseased to bring to Him. No, they gathered the sick and diseased *when they had knowledge of Him.*

What did the men of Gennesaret have knowledge of? The Bible said they had knowledge of *Jesus,* and it caused them to gather the sick and diseased and bring them to Him.

Well, what did they know about Him? Jesus must have said to them the same thing He said in Luke chapter 4 when He was reading from the Book of Isaiah in the Old Testament. In other words, Jesus must have said to the men of Gennesaret, *"The Spirit of the Lord is upon me, because he hath anointed me to preach the gospel to the poor; he hath sent me to heal the brokenhearted, to preach deliverance to the captives, and recovering of sight to the blind, to set at liberty them that are bruised, To preach the acceptable year of the Lord"* (Luke 4:18,19; *see* also Isa. 61:1-3).

You see, because Jesus said that to the men of Gennesaret, they had knowledge of Him that He was anointed. So they gathered up the diseased people and besought Him that they might *"only touch the hem of his garment . . ."* (Matt. 14:36). And as many as touched the hem of His garment were healed. They were made perfectly whole!

It was the same way concerning the woman with the issue of blood. When she had *heard of Jesus,* she *"came in the press behind, and touched his garment"* (Mark 5:27). When she did that, she was made perfectly well, and Jesus said to her, *"Daughter, thy faith hath made thee whole"* (v. 34).

What made the woman go to Jesus in the first place? It says, *"When she had HEARD OF JESUS"* (Mark 5:27).

Now for her to have *heard* about Jesus, somebody had to have *told* her about Jesus. And I'm sure of this one thing: They told her Jesus was anointed by the Spirit of God to minister. And she believed it!

So you see, your faith has something to do with your receiving healing through the healing anointing. You cooperate with the anointing through your faith.

FAITH ACTIVATES THE POWER!

Let me give you an illustration along this line. In March 1971, I was preaching in Tyler, Texas, in the grand ballroom of the old Carlton Hotel. After ministering one night and sending folks to the prayer room to be saved, we invited the sick to come forward to be prayed for.

When I called for folks to get in the healing line, I noticed a lady sitting right in the front, in the first couple of rows. But this woman couldn't get up. Her husband was trying without much success to help her get up.

Finally, one of the ushers helped, and the two men together got her to her feet. She had a cane in one hand, and with her husband holding her by one arm and the usher holding her by the other arm, she slowly made her way into the healing line.

The people were lined up straight across the room, and I went down the line, laying hands upon them. Well, when I laid hands on her, it was just like I had laid hands on a doorknob—there was no receptivity on her part whatsoever.

I went on down the line, laying hands on folks and praying. I didn't have time to stop and preach her a sermon. I knew that in her case, it was a matter of her not having faith. You see, faith *receives. When* you pray, you believe you *receive*! The Bible says that *then*—after you believe you receive—you shall have whatever it is you were desiring (Mark 11:24).

Believing is receiving. Receiving is believing. If there is no receiving, then there's been no believing. If there's no believing, then there is no receiving. It's just that simple—so simple, we stumble over the simplicity of it.

I finished the healing line in that meeting in Tyler and went back to the platform to get my Bible, my notebook, and my watch. This crippled woman was still standing there with her husband by her side to hold her up.

With great effort and with her husband's help, she moved a little closer to me and said, "Brother Hagin, I want you to lay hands on me again."

I remembered when I laid hands on her a few moments before, there was just no response. So I said, "Well, I've already laid hands on you," and then I tried to encourage her to believe. You see, she had a part to play in receiving her healing.

Then she said to me, "This is the very first time I've ever been in one of these kinds of meetings. I'm Presbyterian, and I've never been to a meeting like this. But I'll tell you why I came.

"I have arthritis," she explained. "That's the reason I couldn't get up out of my seat. That's why my body is so stiff."

She continued: "But I saw one of my neighbors walking down the street this afternoon. She was just about as bad off with arthritis as I am—maybe worse. I knew she couldn't walk, yet there she was walking down the street perfectly, with nobody helping her!

"I sent my husband to go get her so I could talk to her. I thought she'd gotten hold of some new medicine somewhere or found some doctor who was an expert with arthritis.

"I asked her about it, and she said, 'No, I was just down there at the grand ballroom of the Carlton Hotel last night. And a minister laid his hands on me, and the Lord healed me instantly. I fell on the floor, and when I got up, the arthritis was gone.'

"When she told me that," this woman continued, "I said to my husband, 'Well, you just get me down there; we'll have that minister lay hands on me too.'

"That's why I came tonight. I came here to try you out to see what you could do."

I said, "Well, you found out what *I* could do, didn't you?"

"Yes," she said, "*nothing.*"

You see, so many times that's the case. Folks just want to see what the *minister* can do instead of believing God for themselves and believing in His power.

LEARN TO BELIEVE GOD FOR YOURSELF

Then this woman said to me: "In this meeting, I heard you say that the Lord appeared to you."

"Well," I said, "He did appear to me. I'd be lying if I said He didn't."

She said, "I heard you say that He laid the finger of His right hand in the palm of each one of your hands."

I said, "He sure did. A fellow would go to hell for lying just as quick as he would for stealing. And I'd be lying if I said Jesus didn't lay the finger of His right hand in the palm of each one of my hands."

She continued: "I heard you say that Jesus told you to tell us that if we'd believe that and receive it, then that same anointing would flow from your hands into our bodies and drive out the sickness and disease."

I answered, "I said that, all right. Jesus told me to say it. If I said He didn't, I'd be lying about it."

"Well," she said, "I'll tell you, I'm ready to believe it. Just put your hand on me."

I could see that she was ready. I could see her earnestness, so I just reached out toward her, and, really, I barely touched her. I barely brushed her forehead with my hand, and I was conscious of the anointing just rushing into her. You see, she pulled it out of me, and it just rushed into her.

Then she fell backward onto the floor and lay there for a little bit. When she made an effort to get up, her husband and another lady nearby helped her. When she got up, her husband tried to hand her that cane. She pulled away from it and said, "Can't you see I don't need that?" Her body was just as limber and free as mine was—all the arthritis had disappeared! Every bit of it was gone, glory to God!

Well now, what activated that power or anointing? Faith did. *Faith activates the power!*

Now I was anointed with that healing power the first time I laid hands on the woman. In fact, although I didn't tell her, the anointing on me was stronger when I laid hands on her the first time than it was the second time when she finally received.

Well, why didn't that anointing heal her the first time? Because she came to the meeting to see what *I* could do—to try me out. But when she put her faith in *God* and *His* power, and she *acted upon* her faith, she received her healing. Why? Because faith activates the power!

Remember Jesus said to the woman with the issue of blood, "Daughter, *thy faith* hath made thee whole." Her faith in God and His power is what activated the anointing on her behalf to drive out her disease and heal her.

MAKE A DEMAND ON THAT 'HEAVENLY ELECTRICITY'!

On another occasion, I was preaching in a certain church in Jacksboro, Texas. It was in December 1950, after Jesus had appeared to me in the vision in September.

The building was so full during that meeting that the pastor had all the visiting ministers sit on the platform. About fourteen ministers had come to visit the meeting. (When things start happening in meetings and God is manifesting Himself, folks get interested.)

In one particular service, a young man in his mid- to late-twenties got in the healing line. As a matter of fact, he got in the healing line every single night. I think I laid hands on him fourteen or fifteen times—maybe more!

And every time I laid hands on him, it was just—*yuck*. Do you know what I mean by "yuck"? I mean, it was like laying hands on a doorknob. There was no receptivity whatsoever.

So when this fellow came in the healing line again the next night, I said to myself, "Here comes that poor fellow again. If he hasn't changed his thinking, he's not going to get a thing from the Lord."

Well, I couldn't just pass him by without laying hands on him because I didn't want to hurt his feelings. I thought maybe if I could keep him coming to the services, I might be able to get faith into him eventually and he might receive something. So I wanted to be very careful with him and not simply turn him away.

I thought, "Well, I'll just go ahead and lay hands on him and pray with him. That will at least satisfy him that I took a little time with him. He's not going to get anything anyway. I'll just pray for him and send him on his way."

But what I didn't know was that this young man had changed his thinking! He'd come to this service *believing*! I didn't know that at the time. The pastor told me all about it afterward, but I'm going to tell you ahead of time so you can better understand what happened.

You remember I said this occurred in December 1950. In December it gets dark earlier in the day than at other times of the year.

Well, the parsonage was next door to the church. The pastor was responsible for turning the church lights on at night before the people started coming for the evening services.

The pastor told me, "Before the meeting tonight, I went over to the church earlier than usual to turn on the lights. I stepped up on the front steps of the church, but before I reached the lights, I stumbled over someone. It was dark, and when I finally got the lights on, I realized it was this young man. He was just sitting there on the front steps in the dark, all wrapped up in a blanket to keep himself warm.

"The young man got up and came inside the church with me. The first thing he said to me was, 'Pastor, you just watch—tonight, the minute Brother Hagin touches me, I'll receive.'"

That reminds me of the woman with the issue of blood in Mark chapter 5. It said, *"When she had heard of Jesus, came in the press behind, and touched his garment. For she SAID, If I may touch but his clothes, I SHALL BE WHOLE"* (vv. 27–28).

So when this young man came in the healing line that night, I reached out to touch his forehead. But, you know, I never really did touch him. I only got my hand within a couple inches of his head when fire jumped out of my hand and hit that young man right in the forehead. All fourteen of the ministers sitting on the platform saw it. In fact, one of them said to me afterward, "I never would have believed it if I hadn't seen it for myself."

Everyone else in the building saw it too. When that fire hit him, it made a popping sound. Well, did you ever notice that many times fire is spoken of in connection with the Holy Ghost?

You see, when I reached out to lay my hand on that young man, he "jerked" that Holy Ghost power out of me with his faith. It almost felt like electricity in the natural realm. I mean, I saw stars!

The healing anointing—God's "electricity" in the supernatural realm—works in much the same way that electricity does in the natural realm.

For example, have you ever grabbed hold of a live electric wire? I have. Once I was emptying a tub of water, and the ground was damp all around me. Afterward, I reached up to turn off the light. It was an old-fashioned light, and I had to touch the metal near the bulb to turn it off.

Well, when I touched the metal part of that bulb, it just sort of grabbed me. It grabbed my hand, and I couldn't turn loose of the thing! The gravity of my own body weight, which was only about 110 pounds at the time, finally pulled me loose.

Because of the wet ground beneath me, my hand had just stuck to that fixture. I could almost see fire coming out of my eyes, and my body jumped and jerked for a few seconds. I could even feel my teeth rattling. Finally, I fell to the ground, but my hand burned for days afterwards.

Well, that was sort of the way it was when I reached out to lay hands on that young man. So much of that heavenly electricity was jerked out of me that I almost fell off the platform!

You see, that manifestation was just the beginning of things like that happening in my ministry. And we didn't have anyone present like we do today to catch folks who fall under the power of God. That's because nobody was falling in those days! It wasn't until about 1952 that people started falling on a regular basis under the power of God in my ministry.

But here's something else that happened. When I reached out to touch that young man and the fire hit him, the power of God picked that fellow up in front of all of us, turned him over to a horizontal position, and held him suspended in midair! (Some people get excited about folks falling on the *floor* under God's power—but just wait till they start falling backward and lying in the *air*!)

Then after the power of God suspended that young man in midair, it sort of threw him underneath the front pew. He went rolling under that front pew like a log!

That young man had gotten his thinking and his believing straightened out. He believed in God and His power. Then he acted on his faith when he said to the pastor, "You just watch. Tonight, as soon as Brother Hagin touches me, I'll receive." And he did, hallelujah! That young man received a powerful manifestation of the anointing!

I'm really expecting more things like that to happen in this day and time. I believe we're right on the verge of it. I believe as we learn more about the anointing, and *expect* God to manifest Himself, He will, and we'll see marvelous results and benefits through faith and the anointing.

—Chapter 3—

Tap Into the Healing Flow!

We have talked briefly about the healing anointing or the power of God and about certain spiritual laws that govern the operation of this power. We also discussed the importance of faith in activating the power and receiving healing through the healing anointing.

In this chapter, we're going to continue our study along the lines of activating the anointing and tapping into the healing flow of God's divine power.

As I said before, many times we have formed our own opinion of how we thought the anointing should work. But the only way to find out how this anointing to heal operates and how it is activated is just simply to study the ministry of Jesus and see what happened concerning the healing anointing in His ministry.

The Woman With the Issue of Blood Tapped Into the Healing Flow

We've already read the account of the woman with the issue of blood in Mark chapter 5. But Mark's Gospel gives a clear, concise picture of Jesus' ministering with the anointing and how the anointing works.

MARK 5:25-30

25 And a certain woman, which had an issue of blood twelve years,

26 And had suffered many things of many physicians, and had spent all that she had, and was nothing bettered, but rather grew worse,

27 When she had heard of Jesus, came in the press behind, and touched his garment.

28 For she said, If I may touch but his clothes, I shall be whole.

29 And straightway the fountain of her blood was dried up; and she felt in her body that she was healed of that plague.

30 And Jesus, immediately knowing in himself that VIRTUE HAD GONE OUT OF HIM . . . .

The *King James Version* said "virtue" had gone out of Jesus. Well, Jesus wasn't anointed with *virtue*; He was anointed with *power*! In most translations, the word "power" is used instead of *virtue*. Even some margins of the *King James Version* list the word "power" as another word for *virtue*.

Now we realize that the New Testament wasn't written in English; it was written in Greek. And the Greek word for virtue in Mark 5:30 is *dunamis* and is translated as "power" in other places throughout the New Testament. That's where we get our English word "dynamite."

Power went out of Jesus when the woman with the issue of blood touched the hem of His garment! It was "dynamite" power! So it wouldn't do any harm to the scripture to read Mark 5:30 this way: "Jesus, immediately knowing in Himself that *power* had gone out of Him . . . ."

Let's look again at the text in Mark 5.

MARK 5:30-34

30 And Jesus, immediately knowing in himself that VIRTUE [power] had gone out of him, turned him about in the press, and said, Who touched my clothes?

31 And his disciples said unto him, Thou seest the multitude thronging thee, and sayest thou, Who touched me?

32 And he looked round about to see her that had done this thing.

33 But the woman fearing and trembling, knowing what was done in her, came and fell down before him, and told him all the truth.

34 And he said unto her, Daughter, thy faith hath made thee whole; go in peace, and be whole of thy plague.

In this passage, we see that Jesus ministered to an individual. The power flowed out of Him and into the woman. Matthew and Luke also tell the same account; however, Mark goes into more detail about it.

The healing of the woman with the issue of blood is a personal testimony of an individual who was healed under Jesus' ministry. There were many individuals who were healed under Jesus' ministry, and there were many cases in which a *crowd* or a *multitude* was healed. But not every one of those cases has a detailed testimony. The Bible just says, "He was healed" or "They were healed." In other words, it just tells about the healing in a word or two.

But there's a personal testimony connected to this account of the woman with the issue of blood. The Bible tells us about the woman—how long she'd had the disease, the fact that she'd suffered many things of many physicians, and the fact that the doctors had given up on her case. It also tells us she became worse instead of better, but then she heard about Jesus. So you see, there's a testimony to this account.

Verse 30 says power had gone out of Jesus. But what caused that power to go out of Him? That healing power or the anointing didn't just flow out to anybody and everybody. For example, Mark 5 says a multitude was present, thronging or crowding around Jesus. A multitude was touching Jesus, pressing in round about Him, yet the power didn't flow out to them.

But when the woman pressed in through the crowd and touched the hem of Jesus' garment, the power did flow out to her. Jesus asked, "Who touched My clothes?" The disciples answered Jesus, *"Thou seest the MULTITUDE THRONGING THEE . . . "* (v. 31).

So we know the anointing didn't flow out from Jesus just because somebody touched Him, because a multitude was thronging Him and the power didn't flow out of Jesus and into them. Then what caused the power to flow out of Jesus and into this woman? The Bible said it was her *faith.* Jesus said, *"Daughter, thy FAITH hath made thee whole"* (v. 34).

THE ANOINTING WILL WORK FOR AN INDIVIDUAL OR FOR A WHOLE CROWD

Out of the more than fifteen or twenty documentations of healings under the ministry of Jesus in the four Gospels, this account of the woman with the issue of blood is the only one that specifically talks about the power or virtue or the *healing anointing* flowing out of Jesus to heal an *individual.*

Yet on the other hand, it is either stated or implied *many* times that power flowed from Jesus into the sick and *they*—multitudes or crowds—were made well. For instance, it is recorded in the scriptures about the multitude that sought to touch Jesus or to touch His clothes so they could be healed.

MATTHEW 14:34-36

34 And when they [Jesus and His disciples] were gone over, they came into the land of Gennesaret.

35 And when the men of that place had knowledge of him, they sent out into all that country round about, and brought unto him all that were diseased;

36 And besought him that they might ONLY TOUCH THE HEM OF HIS GARMENT: and as many as touched were made perfectly whole.

You see, it doesn't say anything in this passage about power flowing out of Jesus. But when you understand that the other scriptures we read revealed a release of His power, you can see that this must have happened here too. Why else would they want to touch the hem of Jesus' garment? They wanted to touch the hem of His garment because healing power flowed out from it!

Besides this passage in Matthew 14, there is another reference in Luke's Gospel that talks about the healing virtue or power that flowed from Jesus to heal a multitude.

LUKE 6:17-19

17 And he [Jesus] came down with them, and stood in the plain, and the company of his disciples, and a great multitude of people out of all Judaea and Jerusalem, and from the sea coast of Tyre and Sidon, which came to hear him, and to be healed of their diseases;

18 And they that were vexed with unclean spirits: and they were healed.

19 And the whole multitude sought to touch him: FOR THERE WENT VIRTUE OUT OF HIM, and healed them all.

Verse 19 says, *"there went VIRTUE out of him."* In other words, there went "dunamis" or *power* out of Jesus, and the whole multitude was healed!

This passage of scripture in Luke 6 talks about a multitude. And Mark 5 talks about just one woman. But, you see, one individual can tap into the healing anointing by faith or a whole crowd can tap into that power by faith.

Now I want you to notice again, however, that faith is involved. Notice Matthew 14:35 said, *"WHEN the men of that place had KNOWLEDGE of him . . . ."*

You see, you can't believe beyond actual knowledge. That's where so many people miss it. They try to believe beyond their knowledge of the Word. Actually, faith begins where the will of God is known. It says, *"When* they had knowledge of Jesus, they came to Him seeking to touch the hem of His garment" (Matt. 14:35–36).

Well, what did they know about Him? They knew that Jesus was anointed! He must have read from Isaiah the same scriptures He read previously in His hometown of Nazareth (Luke 4:16-21): *"The Spirit of the Lord is upon me, because he hath anointed me . . ."* (v. 18).

Jesus must have said to them, "I'm anointed to preach and to heal." So they had knowledge of Him *that He was anointed.*

When they had knowledge of Jesus, they believed what they'd heard, and they *"brought unto him all that were diseased; And besought him that they might only touch the hem of his garment: and as many as touched were made perfectly whole"* (Matt. 14:35–36).

UNBELIEF WILL STOP THE FLOW OF GOD'S POWER

Now in Luke 4, Jesus read that same passage of scripture from Isaiah, saying that He was anointed to preach and to heal. Then He said to those in the synagogue, *"This day is this scripture fulfilled in your ears"* (Luke 4:21). But they didn't believe it. And so, the Word of God said that He could there do no mighty work.

MARK 6:1–6

1 And he went out from thence, and came into his own country; and his disciples follow him.

2 And when the sabbath day was come, he began to teach in the synagogue: and many hearing him were astonished, saying . . . .

3 Is not this the carpenter, the son of Mary, the brother of James, and Joses, and of Juda, and Simon? and are not his sisters here with us? AND THEY WERE OFFENDED AT HIM.

4 But Jesus said unto them, A prophet is not without honour, but in his own country, and among his own kin, and in his own house.

5 AND HE COULD THERE DO NO MIGHTY WORK, save that he laid his hands upon a few sick folk, and healed them.

6 And he marvelled because of their unbelief.

Someone asked, "Well, if Jesus was anointed with this healing power, why didn't the power just work anyway, whether anyone believed or not?"

Notice it didn't say, "Jesus *would* there do no mighty work." It said, "Jesus *could* there do no mighty work." Even though Jesus was anointed to heal, He *couldn't* heal.

Now why?

MARK 6:6

6   And he marvelled because of their UNBELIEF.

Unbelief stopped the flow of the power!

In Mark chapter 5, Jesus didn't say to the woman with the issue of blood, "Woman, your unbelief has made you whole." I mean, if that were the case, everybody who was in unbelief would be made whole! But, no, Jesus said, "Your *faith* has made you whole; go in peace and be whole of thy plague" (v. 34).

Notice again Luke 6:17.

LUKE 6:17

17   And he [Jesus] came down with them, and stood in the plain, and the company of his disciples, and a great multitude of people out of all Judaea and Jerusalem, and from the sea coast of Tyre and Sidon, which came TO HEAR him, and TO BE HEALED of their diseases.

Now I want you to notice that although faith is not specifically spoken of here in this verse, it is inferred. Why? Because it says they came to *hear* Him and to be healed.

Well, we know, of course, that the Bible tells us that faith comes by hearing and hearing by the Word of God (Rom. 10:17). But now, what did those people in Luke 6 hear? They must have heard Jesus read the same scripture, *"The Spirit of the Lord is upon me, because he hath anointed me . . ."* (Luke 4:18). They must have heard Him say, *"This day is this scripture fulfilled in your ears"* (Luke 4:21).

There is a close connection between *believing* what Jesus said and *receiving* from Him. I remember something that Jesus said to me when He appeared to me in that first vision in 1950 in Rockwall, Texas. After Jesus laid the finger of His right hand in the palm of each one of my hands and they began to burn just like I was holding a coal of fire, He said to me, "Kneel down before Me."

I knelt before Him, and He laid His hand on my head and said, "I have called thee and have anointed thee and have given unto thee a special anointing to minister to the sick."

Then He said, "Stand upright on thy feet." I stood up and He said, "This is the primary way you are to minister."

You understand, of course, that ministering by the anointing isn't the only way to minister to the sick. (We'll talk about different ways of ministering and how I've ministered in different ways in the past.) But Jesus said to me, "This is the primary way that you are to minister."

'TELL THE PEOPLE WHAT I'VE TOLD YOU'

Then Jesus said to me, "However, this anointing will not work unless you tell the people exactly what I've told you. Tell them that you saw Me. Tell them I spoke to you. Tell them I laid the finger of My right hand in the palm of each one of your hands. Tell them the healing anointing is in your hands.

"Tell them that I told you to tell them that if they'll believe that, then that power will flow from your hands into their bodies and will drive out their sickness or disease and will effect a healing and a cure in them."

Jesus said the anointing with which He anointed me would not work unless I told that to the people and they believed that I was anointed. Well, we want the anointing to work, don't we?

When Jesus told me that, He was telling me something that was absolutely foreign to my thinking, and He upended some of my theology. (Sometimes, we need our theology upended—and sometimes just thrown completely away—because we've built up what I call religious air castles.)

You see, I'd heard preached, first among the Baptists and then even among the Pentecostals, that Jesus went around healing everybody everywhere He went. Everybody, under all circumstances, was healed under Jesus' ministry. He healed everybody just to prove His divinity or deity. And I believed that because I didn't understand how the healing anointing worked. So what Jesus told me upended my theology.

Jesus also said to me in that vision, "The reason I want you to tell the people what I told you is so they can believe it and have faith. If they don't believe, then they'll not receive."

Jesus continued, "You see, under My own ministry, those who did not receive the *teaching* and the *preaching* did not receive the *healing.*"

Up until then, I thought everybody got healed under Jesus' ministry whether they believed anything or not. I'd heard people say, and I even said it myself, "One thing about it, if you had been there when Jesus walked on the earth, you could have gotten healed."

But everyone didn't get healed under Jesus' ministry when He walked on the earth. For instance, they didn't in Nazareth, Jesus' hometown.

When Jesus said that to me, it came as a revelation. I mean, it floored me! Of course, if you examine the scripture, you know it's right. (And I wouldn't accept a vision or anything else if it didn't line up with the Bible. I don't care if Jesus was standing there talking to me; I still wouldn't accept it if it didn't line up with the Bible.)

Then Jesus said to me in the vision, "You see, I did not minister the way most people think I did."

Actually, He might as well have said, "I did not minister the way *you* think I did," because, really, that's the way I thought He had ministered. I thought everyone just automatically got healed under Jesus' ministry. But He was nice about it and said, "I did not minister the way most people think I did."

Jesus explained: "If I had ministered healing like most people thought I did, then there in Nazareth, I would have said to them,

'Now get five or six blind people.' I would have gotten some of the doctors together—you see, there were doctors then; Luke was a physician—and I would have said, 'Now we'll have these doctors certify that these people are blind.'

"Then I would have said, 'Now go get five or six deaf and mute people, and we'll have the doctors certify that they are deaf and mute. Then get several leprous people, and we'll have the doctors examine them and certify that they have leprosy. Then get several people who are totally paralyzed and bedfast. We'll have the doctors examine them to certify that they are paralyzed. Then I'll just prove to you who I am. I'll just heal them all right now in front of you.'

"But," Jesus continued, "instead of doing that, I got run out of town."

Then Jesus said, "Read the fourth chapter of Luke and you'll find out exactly how I ministered. The first thing I always did when I went into the synagogue or into a city was preach the same sermon. I always read from Isaiah" (Luke 4:17–19).

ISAIAH 61:1-2

1   The Spirit of the Lord God is upon me; because the Lord hath anointed me to preach good tidings unto the meek; he hath sent me to bind up the brokenhearted, to proclaim liberty to the captives, and the opening of the prison to them that are bound;

2   To proclaim the acceptable year of the Lord . . . .

Evidently, whether it was just out in the open or in a synagogue, Jesus took the same text for His first service.

Somebody said, "Are you sure?"

Well, Jesus said He did. I mean, do you know that He *didn't*? We do know from Luke chapter 4 that it was the first sermon He preached in Nazareth.

So Jesus always took His text from Isaiah and said, "The Spirit of the Lord is upon Me." Jesus was a preacher and a teacher, so what would He preach and teach from? From a mail-order catalog? No! And He couldn't have read "The Spirit of the Lord is upon Me" from the New Testament; they didn't have a New Testament then. Any text He took at all would have to have been from the Old Testament.

So Jesus said to me, "I always took My text from Isaiah, and I always read to them, 'The Spirit of the Lord is upon Me, because He's anointed Me.' And then I would say, 'This day is this scripture fulfilled in your ears.'

"Those who would believe it received from Me. Those who wouldn't believe it, didn't."

You see, that's what those people heard who came to hear Jesus (Luke 5:15; 6:17). That's the knowledge they gained of Him. And the scripture said that when they had knowledge of Him, they brought the diseased and sick to be healed. They didn't run Him out of town. No, they went around gathering up all the diseased people, and those people sought to touch the hem of Jesus' garment. And as many as touched Him were healed—every single one of them!

The multitude didn't dispense with Jesus, blessed be God. They came and were healed! But there in His hometown of Nazareth, they began to say, *"From whence hath this man these things? and what wisdom is this which is given unto him, that even such mighty works are wrought by his hands? Is not this the carpenter, the son of Mary, the brother of James, and Joses, and of Juda, and Simon? and are not his sisters here with us? AND THEY WERE OFFENDED AT HIM"* (Mark 6:2–3).

In Nazareth when Jesus said, *"The Spirit of the Lord is upon me"* (Luke 4:18), the people did not accept Him. We can readily see that in verse 28.

LUKE 4:28
28 And all they in the synagogue, when they heard these things, were filled with WRATH.

It says they were filled with wrath. Now they could have been filled with *faith*, because it says that "all they in the synagogue" *heard* Jesus. And we know that faith cometh by hearing, and hearing by the Word of God (Rom. 10:17). So they all could have been filled with faith. But instead, they were filled with wrath. In other words, they got mad about it.

Religious people get mad about things when you don't agree with them. If you say something that's different than what they believe, they get mad. But Spirit-filled people have a teachable spirit.

LUKE 4:28–29

28 And all they in the synagogue, when they heard these things, were filled with wrath,

29 And rose up, and thrust him out of the city, and led him unto the brow of the hill whereon their city was built [if you've ever been to Nazareth, you know exactly what this is talking about], that they might cast him down headlong.

Well, Jesus got run out of town. That's the way He paraphrased it to me: "You know, I got run out of My hometown."

Now why didn't the people get healed there in Nazareth like they did elsewhere? Because they didn't accept the message. They didn't believe when Jesus said, "I'm anointed to heal." The Bible said, *"And he could there do no mighty work, save that he laid his hands upon a few sick folk, and healed them. And he marvelled because of their unbelief"* (Mark 6:5–6).

You can see why Jesus said to me in that vision in Rockwall, Texas, in 1950, "This anointing will not work unless you tell the people that you saw Me and tell them what I told you."

Well, we want the anointing to work, don't we? So if I'm going to minister with the healing anointing, then I have to do what Jesus said.

You understand I can minister anytime in faith and lay hands on people by faith. The Bible already tells me to do that: *"they shall lay hands on the sick, and they shall recover"* (Mark 16:18). I used to do that as a Baptist pastor because I wasn't specially anointed to minister to the sick at that time. But if I'm going to minister with the healing anointing, and that's the primary way I minister now, it won't work unless I tell the people what Jesus told me to tell them: "Tell them you saw Me. Tell them I spoke to you. Tell them

I appeared to you. Tell them I laid the finger of My right hand in the palm of each one of your hands. Tell them the healing anointing is in your hands."

"Well," somebody said, "I'm going to get in Brother Hagin's healing line and try that out to see if it works." It won't. That's doubt and unbelief, and it won't work. You have to believe to receive.

BELIEVE AND RECEIVE

Jesus said, "Tell them that I told you to tell them that if they'll believe you are anointed and will receive that anointing, then that power will flow out of your hands into their body and will drive out their sickness or disease and effect a healing and a cure in them."

Let's go back to Mark chapter 5.

MARK 5:34
34 And he said unto her, Daughter, THY FAITH hath made thee whole; go in peace, and be whole of thy plague.

Then it was the woman's faith, not Jesus' faith, that activated the anointing that Jesus was anointed with!

THE FAITH OF THE CROWD CAN HELP OR HINDER THE ANOINTING

In my years of ministry, I have noticed that when a crowd gets "with" the preacher, teacher, or singer, the anointing is much stronger. The preacher preaches better! The teacher teaches better! And the singer sings better, and helps lead the congregation into the Presence of God. (If you dedicate your talent of singing to the Lord, He can use it and anoint it. Singing is a ministry just like the ministry of the teacher and preacher is a ministry.) But if the crowd is sort of "anti-" whatever you're doing they're not with you, boy, it's tough sledding!

So you see, in some places where Jesus went, the crowd was "with" Him when He started talking about, "I'm anointed." In other words, they didn't pull against Him. They believed Him and just started gathering up the sick folks, saying, "Boy, let's get them in on this!"

But in other places, when Jesus said, "I'm anointed," they got mad about it, rose up, and ran Him out of town. Isn't that what the Bible says?

We need to establish the fact that the anointing, the healing power of God, doesn't just flow out promiscuously, so to speak. In other words, it doesn't just flow out to anybody. Why? Because *faith* activates the power! So you see, the faith of the crowd can help or hinder the anointing.

There was a crowd present where the woman with the issue of blood was. A multitude was there, but she was the only one whom the Word records that got healed. How do I know there was a crowd present? Because the scripture plainly tells us that Jesus was on His way to Jairus' house at the time she pressed through the *crowd* to touch the hem of Jesus' garment (Mark 5:22–27).

YOUR FAITH DETERMINES YOUR OUTCOME

Jesus was momentarily detained by the woman's touching His garment. Then you remember that men came from Jairus' house and said to Jairus, "Your little daughter is dead; don't trouble the Master anymore" (Mark 5:35).

Jesus turned to Jairus and said, "Fear not; only believe" (v. 36). And Jesus proceeded immediately to Jairus' house. In other words, Jesus didn't stop and have a healing service after the woman with the issue of blood was healed. He didn't stop and minister to the crowd who was thronging Him. He proceeded immediately to Jairus' house, and the little maiden was raised up from the dead and was healed (vv. 41–42).

Then the scripture tells us that Jesus went from Jairus' house, and as He departed, two blind men followed Him.

MATTHEW 9:27–28

27 And when Jesus departed thence [from Jairus' house], two blind men followed him, crying, and saying, Thou son of David, have mercy on us.

28 And when he was come into the house . . . .

The house referred to in verse 28 is the house Jesus went to when He came from Jairus' house. Jairus was a ruler of the synagogue in Capernaum. Before reaching Capernaum, Jesus had come back across the Sea of Galilee from the country of the Gadarenes, where the maniac of Gadara had been delivered. When Jesus landed at Capernaum, Jairus met Him.

Then evidently, from what I can gather, Jesus went to Peter's house from Jairus' house. And it says the two blind men came right into the house.

MATTHEW 9:28

28 And when he was come into the house, the blind men came to him: and Jesus saith unto them, BELIEVE YE THAT I AM ABLE TO DO THIS? They said unto him, Yea, Lord.

You see, it seems that Jesus wasn't able to heal folks unless they believed He could.

MATTHEW 9:29–30

29 Then touched he their eyes, saying, ACCORDING TO YOUR FAITH be it unto you.

30 And their eyes were opened . . . .

Notice verse 29: *"According to your faith be it unto you."* According to *whose* faith? *My* faith? *Your* faith? *Jesus'* faith? No, it was the *two blind men's* faith! They tapped into the healing flow! They made a demand by faith on the healing power with which Jesus was anointed, and they activated that power on their behalf.

THE POWER IS PRESENT, BUT YOU MUST TAP INTO THE POWER!

We read in a previous chapter that John G. Lake said, "Electricity is God's power in the natural realm; Holy Ghost power is God's power in the spirit realm." You see, *just like electricity is in existence in the natural world, the power of God is in existence in the spiritual world. And it's a tangible substance!*

Well, just as there are laws that govern the operation of electricity in the natural realm, there are laws and rules that govern the operation of spiritual power too. But I think in times past, we have thought that if the anointing was present, it would automatically manifest itself and just work automatically. But that's not so.

Electricity has been in existence in the earth ever since God created the universe. Then why didn't electricity just automatically light up a house, cook a meal, or warm or cool a house? Because for many years, man didn't even know electricity existed. And even if that electricity did flow right into a house, there was nothing for it to connect with, such as a lamp, a stove, a heater, or an air conditioner, to operate effectually. In other words, the house wasn't equipped for electricity.

In modern time, Benjamin Franklin discovered some of the secrets of harnessing and using electricity that are still being utilized today. Other people played a part in discovering electricity, some as early as 500 B.C. They didn't *invent* or *create* electricity; they began *discovering* its existence. That made it possible over the years for men and women to begin harnessing its power and using it effectually.

But after electricity was discovered and man knew it existed, it didn't just automatically begin to operate. Man had to come in contact with electricity somehow to make it work.

When electricity was discovered, man knew it was a tangible something—an earthly materiality that could be felt. Then why didn't electricity just automatically begin lighting homes? Why didn't it just flow into someone's kitchen and start cooking food!

Why didn't electricity flow into some city or town and make traffic lights start blinking and changing! Because there *weren't* any electric stoves; there *weren't* any traffic lights. Man knew about electricity, but he didn't know what conducts it. He didn't know all about the laws that govern electricity. So he set out to discover them.

Thomas A. Edison did more than any other person to do just that. He was one of the greatest inventors and leaders in industry in history. Think about all the blessings and benefits our modern civilization have enjoyed as a result of his work, particularly here in America.

Well, if we could just get it into our minds that the healing power of God is in existence in the spirit world and that it has laws that govern its operation, too, then men and women would know how to tap into the power and be so blessed by the benefits of the healing anointing!

Someone asked, "If the healing anointing exists, why doesn't it just move on our behalf?"

That's where we've missed it. We've thought, "Well, if it's so, it'll just manifest itself."

No! There's something that has to be done on man's end of the line before there's a manifestation of the healing power. And then a person has to tap into the power by faith.

In the natural, man knew about electricity, all right. It was even manifested in a measure. But man had to learn more about electricity and the laws that governed it before he could fully enjoy it—before he could gain the greatest benefit from it.

It's the same way with God's power—the anointing. That simply means that as we learn more about the anointing and what the Word of God says about it, we will be able to *flow* with the anointing, tap into the power, and gain greater benefits from it as a result.

Another Natural Comparison

We know that the healing anointing can be compared to electricity in the natural realm. The healing anointing is a "heavenly electricity." Another thing about the laws that govern this heavenly substance is this fact: The thing that turns the heavenly power on in the spiritual realm can be compared to an electrical switch on a wall that turns on the earthly power, *electricity*, in the natural realm.

In the natural, when you turn on a switch, electricity flows right into the lighting fixtures and lightens a room. And when you turn the switch off, the lights go out. So in the spiritual realm, the thing that turns on the heavenly power could be called the switch of *faith*!

Remember Jesus said to the woman with the issue of blood, *"Daughter THY faith hath made thee whole"* (Mark 5:34). Jesus said *her* faith made her whole. In other words, she had turned on the switch of faith for healing.

KEEP THE SWITCH OF FAITH TURNED ON!

We read in Acts 19 that the Apostle Paul was anointed with the heavenly power or anointing and that *"from his body were brought unto the sick handkerchiefs or aprons, and the diseases departed from them, and the evil spirits went out of them"* (v. 12).

We already know that Paul was anointed in a similar manner as Jesus was anointed. And there's no doubt about it—as soon as the diseases departed from those who came in contact with the handkerchiefs of Paul, the bodies of those who were sick started getting well.

Many times people fail to realize that it takes time for bodies to respond after disease has departed from them. Even after the diseases have departed, especially in cancer cases, the symptoms will often persist because damage has already been done to the bodies. Sometimes a person's body is healed instantly, but sometimes it just heals up gradually by itself.

On many occasions, I've ministered to sick people, and I've known that their diseases had departed. Yet the people still had their symptoms for a little while. Sometimes it was ten minutes, an hour, or maybe three days before a person was all right. But I knew all the while that the disease had departed.

People need to be taught properly so they can keep the switch of faith turned on, because if they begin to doubt, the disease will come back.

As I said, when I minister the healing anointing to a person, and he receives the anointing in faith, the healing may be manifested right away or it may not be manifested right away. That's the reason I've said to people, "Keep the switch of faith turned on."

INSTANT AND GRADUAL MANIFESTATIONS

I didn't think up that phrase "Keep the switch of faith turned on" on my own. It just sprung up in my spirit during a meeting my wife and I held several years ago.

The meeting was held in a certain denominational church in which several hundred members of the congregation had received the baptism in the Holy Ghost and turned Charismatic! We laid hands on the sick each night during the meeting, and one particular night, there was a blind woman in the healing line. I laid hands on her, and she fell on the floor under the power of God. When she got up, you didn't have to ask her if she received. Her face was lit up like a neon sign in the dark, and she was shouting, "I can see! I can see!"

We learned later that she'd been blind for three years. She'd been able to detect an object if it was in front of her, but she couldn't tell if it was a man, woman, boy, girl, horse, cow, or automobile. That was pretty blind, wasn't it? But after I laid hands on her, she could see clearly! She was instantly healed!

THE BABY WITH DEFORMED FEET

That same night, a young couple brought their only child to be prayed for. Both of his little feet were clubbed—deformed. I held those little feet in my hands and ministered God's healing power to them. When I opened my eyes, I saw that those feet looked just as crippled as they were to begin with.

I said to the parents, "If it will help you any, I'll tell you this: I have a stronger anointing on me right now than I had when I laid hands on that woman who was blind. I'm just going to hold these little feet in my hands for a few moments." After I did that, those feet looked just as crippled and deformed as they ever were.

Well, what are you going to tell people in a situation like that? I said to them, "All I know is what Jesus told me when He appeared to me in the vision and gave me a special anointing to minister to the sick. He told me, 'When you feel that power go out of your hands into them, you know they're healed.'"

I continued: "I felt that power go out of my hands into the child's feet. So keep the switch of faith turned on. Every time you think of it, say, 'The healing power of God has been ministered to those feet, and the power is working in them right now.'"

That was on a Thursday night, and we closed the meeting on the following Sunday and went on our way. Several months later, the son of the pastor of that church was in one of our meetings. He said, "That couple came back to church the following Sunday, came up to the platform, and asked for the privilege to show the child to the congregation. They held the child up so everyone could see, and both of his feet were perfect!"

Well, that couple kept the switch of faith turned on! This is their testimony:

"We did just what Brother Hagin said to do." (Actually, it wasn't me who said it; it was the Holy Ghost. I didn't even know I was going to say it. It just came up out of my spirit: "Keep the switch of faith turned on.")

This young couple said, "Every time we looked at our son's feet, we'd say, 'Thank God, the healing power of God was ministered to those feet Thursday night, and that power is working in those feet now to effect a healing and a cure.'

"We kept saying that morning and night—every time we thought about it. After three days, his feet started changing. It wasn't instant, but little by little over the next three or four days, they continued to change until they were just as perfect as feet can be!"

Well, Mark 16:18 said, *"they shall lay hands on the sick, and they SHALL RECOVER."* Now that blind woman in my meeting was healed instantly, but the young couple kept the switch of faith turned on, and their son recovered!

So if you get an instant healing, just thank God for it. But if you don't, don't turn off the switch of faith! Keep saying, "The power of God is working in me," and keep the switch of faith turned on.

THE MAN WHO'D NEVER WALKED

Years ago I preached a three-night meeting for a fellow minister, and in one of the services there was a man in his forties who had never walked a step in his life. When I laid hands on this man for healing, I knew that the power of God went into him. I said to the man, "The power went into you."

He said, "I know it. I felt it go all over me like electricity."

I don't usually tell people in wheelchairs to get up out of their wheelchairs unless the Lord tells me to. Usually—almost without exception—when the Lord has directed me to tell people to get up out of their wheelchairs, they were healed instantly.

I just told this man, "The power went into you," and I went on praying for other folks.

Some of the men in the church decided to get this man out of his wheelchair. They held him up and tried to get him to walk. But the minute they turned the man loose, he fell in a heap on the floor. They got him up again and tried to get him to walk, but when they turned him loose, he fell in a heap on the floor. So they put him back in his chair.

On Wednesday, the third night of the meeting, the pastor and I drove up to the church and were still sitting in the car discussing scripture when I looked up and saw a man running up the steps to the church. I didn't recognize him at first, but then the pastor saw him and said, "Look! Look!"

Well, I was already looking in that direction, but I thought, "What is so great about seeing a man run up steps!"

The pastor said, "You didn't recognize him, did you?"

"No," I said, "who was it?"

He said, "That's the man who hadn't walked a step in his life!"

We went into the service, and after the singing and the preliminaries, the pastor said, "Before we turn the service over to Brother Hagin, we want Brother _____ to come up here and testify."

This was the testimony the man gave to the congregation:

"Monday night, Brother Hagin laid hands on me. There wasn't any immediate healing, but he told me that the power had gone into me. He didn't have to tell me—I felt it. It went all over me like electricity. It was like a warm glow that went all over my body."

Then the man said to the congregation, "You saw some of the brethren get me up and try to get me to walk, and I fell on the floor. But I didn't let that discourage me.

"We went home, and one of my brothers took me out of my chair, helped me get on my nightclothes, and picked me up and put me on my bed."

You see, this man could move his arms, but he couldn't walk a step. He couldn't dress or get into bed by himself.

The man said, "I went to sleep saying, 'The healing power of God was ministered to me at church tonight. That power's working in my body now to effect a healing and a cure.'

"I just said that over and over, like a person would count sheep, until I fell asleep.

"The first thing I said when I woke up the next morning was, 'The power of God was ministered to my body last night. That power is working in my body to effect a healing and a cure.'

"My brother came in and got me out of bed. He helped me dress, put me in my chair, and rolled me to the breakfast table. After breakfast, he put me in the den, and I just sat there praising God because the healing power was ministered to my body last night and that power was working in me, effecting a healing and a cure."

He related that when he went to sleep Tuesday night, he said over and over, "The healing power of God was ministered to me last night. It's working in me now to effect a healing and a cure."

He said to the congregation, "I don't know how many times I said that. I went to sleep saying it, and when I woke up this morning, I continued saying, 'The healing power of God was ministered to my body Monday night. That power is in me now to effect a healing and a cure.' I just kept saying it.

"My brother got me out of bed, helped me dress, put me in my wheelchair, and rolled me to the breakfast table. After breakfast, he put me back in the den. The rest of the family went about their business, and I just sat there all morning saying. 'The healing power of God was ministered to me Monday night . . .'

"At about three o'clock this afternoon, as I was saying 'The healing power of God was ministered to me,' I felt strength come to my body, and for the first time in my life, I got up on my own and stood up! I still couldn't walk, but I could stand up on my feet and legs for the first time in my life. But then I grew weak, so I sat down."

(Yet, you see, this man wasn't discouraged. A lot of folks would have gotten over into doubt immediately, saying, "I thought the power was going to work, but it didn't. Poor old me. I don't understand why God didn't heal me." But this man kept the switch of faith turned on!)

The man continued, "I kept saying over and over that the healing power was ministered to me and that it was effecting a healing and cure in my body.

"Then I felt another surge of strength throughout my body, and I felt the urge to get up again. So I stood up—only this time, I started walking! I walked around the den three times, and I've been walking ever since!"

This man knew how to tap into God's healing flow, and he kept the switch of faith turned on!

THE LITTLE NINE-YEAR-OLD GIRL

In January 1951, I was holding a meeting in Beaumont, Texas, and a lady brought her nine-year-old daughter to be prayed for. This was shortly after the Salk vaccine was developed, but this little girl had contracted polio as a baby. As a result, her legs never developed. In fact, her mother had carried this nine-year-old girl to the healing line; the girl couldn't walk.

I took the child out of her mother's arms and set her on my lap. The girl's little limbs looked like pipe stems and flopped like a rag doll. I laid my hands on those deformed limbs, and I felt the power go into her. I felt it leave my hands and go into those little legs.

Now Jesus had said to me, "When that power—that anointing—leaves your hands and goes into the people, you know they're healed." That means, as far as He's concerned, it's done!

As I was ministering to this little girl, I thought about something. This girl was her mother's only child. I had a little girl about the same age, and I had the utmost compassion for this mother.

I said to the congregation, "Reach out your hands toward this little girl. What if this were your child? If it were, you wouldn't just sit there. No, you'd be interested in getting her healed. You'd be participating in her healing."

I said that because that's when things happen—when you get everybody participating.

After that, I said to this little girl's mother, "The healing power was ministered to those limbs in Jesus' Name," and I handed the girl back to her mother—the child's legs just as crippled and deformed as they ever were. The woman took the child and went back to her seat.

The next morning I was shaving in the guest quarters that were adjacent to the parsonage. I heard somebody running up the steps calling my name, and I recognized that it was

Brother _____. He ran in, and I could see that he was elated about something.

"What is it?" I asked.

"Well, do you remember that little girl you prayed for last night who'd had polio?"

"Yes."

"Well, she's over there at the church with her mother, and she's perfectly healed! That little girl is skipping up and down the aisles of the church!"

And sure enough, when we looked at her feet and legs, we saw that they were as perfect as any nine-year-old's!

Here is that mother's testimony:

"After the meeting last night when you prayed for our little girl, my husband put her in the back seat of the car. By the time we got home, she was asleep.

"When I lifted her out of the car, she was seemingly no better. I got her into her nightclothes and put her to bed.

"The next morning, I let her sleep in while I fixed breakfast for my husband. At about eight o'clock, I woke her up, picked her up in my arms, and carried her into the bathroom. I'd already drawn her bathwater, so I removed her nightclothes and sat her in the tub.

"I was there on my knees bathing her, and I began to cry. The tears that poured from my eyes streamed down my cheeks and into the water. I said, 'Oh, Lord, why didn't You heal my baby? I so wanted her to be healed.'"

You see, one of the girl's legs was much shorter than the other one, and it sort of dangled outward like a tentacle. Well, in ten days, doctors were going to pull that leg down and straighten it out and fuse the girl's hip. That procedure is similar to welding. Once they did that, her hip would always be stiff.

The mother continued, "There I was crying beside the tub when something on the inside of me spoke up and said, 'Do you believe Brother Hagin is a man of God?'"

This mother was born again and Spirit-filled. The Holy Spirit is within born-again people, all right. But, I'll tell you, they get into a deeper dimension when they get baptized with the Holy Ghost!

You see, the Holy Spirit was in this woman. It wasn't her spirit that spoke up—it was the Holy Ghost abiding in her spirit who spoke.

He said, "Do you believe Brother Hagin is a man of God?"

"Why, certainly I believe that," she answered.

She related: "That 'Something' spoke to me again and said, 'Do you believe Brother Hagin is a prophet of God?'

"I answered, 'Yes, I believe that too.'

"Then Something on the inside of me said, 'Do you believe that Brother Hagin sat right there on the platform and held your child in his arms and told a lie?'

"I said, 'No, I don't believe he lied.'

"'Well,' that voice said, 'if he didn't lie, then that power was ministered to your child last night.'

"I dried up my tears and said with joy, 'Yes, that's right! I believe the healing power of God was ministered to my child's body last night. I believe that power flowed out of Brother Hagin's hands into her body to effect a healing and a cure.'

"After I said that, I heard something popping. It sounded like dry sticks breaking. I looked down, and right there before my eyes, both of those legs straightened out and grew out to normal size!"

Hundreds of people were witnesses. Hundreds of people saw that girl's new legs who had seen her legs crippled just the night before!

This woman almost lost her daughter's healing because there wasn't an instant manifestation. She started out saying, "Lord, why didn't You heal my baby," but then she turned the switch of faith on! That faith activated the power that had already been ministered to the little girl, and the girl was healed and made whole!

HEALING IS BASED ON TWO CONDITIONS

I have found out that with the greater anointing—when I have a stronger anointing in manifestation—I always have more instant healings. But as I said, healings are not always instant. Many times they are gradual.

Now the reason healing is gradual or by process is that healing is based on two conditions: (1) the degree of healing power or virtue that's administered; (2) the degree of faith that gives *action* to the power or virtue administered.

In other words, it doesn't matter how strongly I'm anointed or how strongly a minister is anointed, if there's no faith to give *action* to the power, there will be no healing.

Let's prove that by the scriptures.

PROVERBS 4:20–22

20 My son, attend to my words; incline thine ear unto my sayings.
21 Let them not depart from thine eyes; keep them in the midst of thine heart.
22 For they [my words] are life unto those that [seek or] find them, and HEALTH to all their flesh.

Now if you have a good reference Bible, you'll notice that next to the word "health" there is a little number or letter. If you look in the margin, it says that the Hebrew word translated "health" also means *medicine*. In other words, that verse is saying, "My Words are *medicine*." Medicine to what? To all their flesh.

I want to ask you a question. Do you know any medicine that you could take one dose of and be instantly, perfectly well? Well, in much the same way, you're not going to take just one dose of the Word and be well.

I know the Bible said, *"He sent his word, and healed them"* (Ps. 107:20). But it also said, "My Words are medicine" (Prov. 4:22). The Word will produce healing in a person's body and become "health to all their flesh," but it is not always instantaneous.

So healing is by degree based on two conditions: (1) the degree of healing virtue administered; (2) the degree of faith that gives *action* to the power or healing virtue administered.

Notice what Jesus said to the woman with the issue of blood in Mark 5. Yes, the power or healing virtue flowed into her. In fact, she was the only one in the crowd the power flowed into. But Jesus said, "Daughter, *thy faith* hath made thee whole" (Mark 5:34).

What caused that power to flow out of Jesus into her? *Her faith!* The woman with the issue of blood learned to tap into the healing flow! Her faith made a demand on the healing power or anointing, and that anointing flowed into her and effected healing "to all her flesh." Her faith made her whole!

Learn to tap into the healing flow of God's power for yourself and then keep the switch of faith turned on. Your faith can make you whole too!

—Chapter 4—

You Can Write Your Own Ticket With God

When she had heard of Jesus, came in the press behind, and touched his garment.

For she said, If I may touch but his clothes, I shall be whole.

And straightway the fountain of her blood was dried up; and she felt in her body that she was healed of that plague.

And Jesus, immediately knowing in himself that virtue had gone out of him, turned him about in the press, and said, Who touched my clothes? . . .

And he looked round about to see her that had done this thing.

But the woman fearing and trembling, knowing what was done in her, came and fell down before him, and told him all the truth.

And he said unto her, Daughter, thy faith hath made thee whole; go in peace, and be whole of thy plague.

—Mark 5:27–30, 32–34

I remember that when Jesus appeared to me in a vision in 1953, I was holding a meeting in a particular church in Phoenix, Arizona. I was scheduled to be there three weeks.

I was staying in the home of some friends, and on the Friday night of the third week of meetings, the folks I was staying with invited their three daughters and sons-in-law over for a time of fellowship after the meeting.

We men were all sitting in the living room, visiting, and the ladies were in the kitchen. They'd prepared some beautiful things to eat, and we were getting ready to eat when, suddenly, I had an urge to pray.

Now I don't mean it was just a leading. You can have a leading to pray sometimes. But this was an overwhelming urge to pray. I don't know whether you can understand that or not. I tell you, sometimes you'll get such an urge and such a burden to pray that it feels like you're going to burst wide open if you don't pray. In other words, you've got to give some kind of expression to the burden you feel.

I think we ought to be wise in this area. For example, if this happens to you and you're around people who don't know about the Holy Ghost and the things of God, you need to be discreet. In my case, if I had been around people like that who didn't know much about the things of God, I wouldn't have done what I did. I would have excused myself, gone to the privacy of my own room, and prayed. But I still would have prayed; I wouldn't have eaten at that time.

But these people were all Full Gospel, Pentecostal people. They understood things about prayer and intercession and the things of the Spirit. So because of the people I was with, I simply said to Brother Fisher, our host, "I've got to pray, and I've got to pray now." Brother Fisher said, "Well, let's pray then." So he called the ladies into the living room, where we all prayed. (We ended up with a cold meal, but after it was all over, nobody wanted to eat anyway. It didn't make us a bit of difference in the world whether we ate or not.)

It was after we "prayed through" that night and got the victory that the Lord appeared to me in a vision and showed me some important steps required in receiving healing, or whatever it is a person needs from God. But before I share with you what He showed me, I'm going to take a side journey that I believe will help you understand some things about the Spirit of God.

Praying in the Spirit in Other Tongues

My wife wasn't with me during this particular meeting in 1953, so it was five men and four ladies who prayed that night in Brother Fisher's living room. We all got down on our knees to pray, and by the time my knees hit the floor, I was in the Spirit.

What do I mean by "in the Spirit"?

I was praying in the Spirit in other tongues; I never did pray one word in English. I was praying in other tongues as fast as I could "rattle it off." And I prayed for forty-five minutes that way. It seemed like I didn't even stop to catch my breath. I mean, it was just rolling out of me. It almost seemed like I didn't have anything to do with it.

Well, I was praying in the Spirit. That's scriptural, because the

Bible said, *"Praying always with all prayer and supplication in the Spirit, and watching thereunto with all perseverance and supplication for all saints"* (Eph. 6:18).

The folks that I was with that night understood "praying in the Spirit." The trouble with people today is that they don't know anything about the Spirit, so they just put their own interpretation on spiritual things.

But, you see, by praying in the Spirit, you gain experience. And you learn by experience what it means to pray in the Spirit in your own language and in other tongues.

Paul referred to this in writing to the Galatians.

GALATIANS 4:19
19 My little children, of whom I TRAVAIL [in the Spirit] in birth again until Christ be formed in you.

Paul was using the term "travail" in the sense of a woman travailing to give birth to a child. He was talking about a spiritual travailing in prayer.

Well, during the forty-five minutes I prayed there in that family's living room, I groaned and cried, and it seemed as if right down in my stomach, in my innermost being, that I was almost going to burst. I mean, it almost hurt.

After a while, I had the victory for whatever I was praying about. Many times you won't know what it is you're praying about. The Holy Ghost won't see fit to tell you. But when you've "prayed through," you just know that victory is forthcoming, because you have a note of praise or thanksgiving.

Usually, I'll begin to sing in other tongues or laugh in the Spirit. And not every time, but once in a while, the Lord will let me see and know who I'm praying for and what I'm praying about. It so happened in this particular case, He let me know that I was praying for an older gentleman who would be coming to the Sunday night service of the meeting.

I'd never seen this man before in my life, but the Lord showed him to me as we were praying. I saw myself ministering. I saw myself closing my sermon and then leaning over the pulpit and pointing to this fellow. I said to him, "The Lord shows me that you're past seventy years of age and that you do not believe there is a hell. You've been raised to believe there is no hell. But the Lord told me to tell you that you've got one foot in hell now, and the other one is slipping in."

Then I saw the gentleman come from where he was sitting and kneel down at the altar and get saved!

Well, on Sunday night Brother Fisher and I located the man. He was sitting exactly where I'd seen him sitting, and was dressed exactly as I'd seen him when I was in the Spirit on Friday night. After I preached my sermon, I acted out what the Lord had shown me, and this gentleman came to the altar and got saved!

Afterward, this man shook hands with us and hugged our necks. He said to the pastor, "That preacher said I was past seventy years of age. I'm seventy-two.

"He also said I was raised to believe that there was no hell. My parents were Universalists; they taught me that there was no hell."

He continued, "This is the first time I've ever been inside a church. And when that preacher said, 'You've got one foot in hell, and the other one is slipping in, I knew exactly what he was talking about. I've had a severe heart attack, and the doctor said my heart is in such a condition that I could die at any moment."

You see, this man could have slipped into hell at any moment. That's what the Lord wanted me to pray about. Who would have ever known to pray for that man? I didn't know he was going to be there in that service. To my knowledge, none of the other church people knew he was going to be there either. But the Holy Ghost knows who's going to be at every service!

Jesus Appeared to Me

Now something else interesting happened after I finished praying for this gentleman that night at the Fishers' house. After I'd prayed and gotten the victory and began laughing in the Spirit, Jesus appeared to me.

I saw Him standing there in front of me just as plainly as I'd seen Brother Fisher and his family there before we began praying.

It was just that real, yet I had my eyes shut, so it was a spiritual vision. A spiritual vision is a vision in which you see with the eyes of your spirit.[1]

In this spiritual vision, Jesus talked to me about my ministry. I'd also recently been praying about finances, and He talked to me about my finances too.

This is what the Lord said to me in the vision: "Fifty-four [He meant 1954—you see, this was a Friday night in December 1953] will be the year for more."

Well, that has a twofold application. For example, many times in the Old Testament, when God said something through the prophets, very often what God said had a twofold meaning. In other words, it had a natural meaning for Israel, and then it had a meaning beyond that time period—for the Church.

For instance, the prophets of old prophesied about Jesus' coming, which happened years later and ushered in the time of the Church and the New Testament or New Covenant.

So when the Lord said, "Fifty-four is the year for more," I understood exactly what He was saying. He was talking, first of all, about my ministry, and second, about my finances. Those were the two things He had talked to me about: ministry and finances.

So that's what He meant—'54 would be a year for more ministry-wise or spiritually. And it was.

He also meant that '54 would be a year for more financially, and it was! I had been out on the field since 1949—about five years. And in that one year's time, in 1954, God did more for me financially than the other four years put together *times two*!

In 1954 the Lord gave me two houses with the lots, plus a brand-new automobile! That isn't bad, especially when you consider I didn't have any of those things before! I mean, they just sort of fell into my lap! There was no struggle about them at all. God had said, "Fifty-four is the year for more"!

Then about my ministry, the Lord said, "Be faithful; fulfill your ministry, for the time is short." Well, if the time was short in 1954, think how much shorter it is now! It's much shorter!

After Jesus said all that to me in this vision, He turned around and walked away, just like someone who's standing in a room might turn and walk out the door into a hallway.

And I said, "Dear Lord, wait just a moment. May I ask You a question, please?"

Now later, after the vision was over, I thought of all kinds of things I wanted to ask Jesus I didn't think of at the time I was standing there with Him face to face. Why didn't I think of them at the time? Because I wasn't operating in the mental realm when Jesus stood there before me. I was operating in the spirit realm. When you're in the spirit realm, whatever is heavy on your spirit or heart is all you think about.

Well, I had something on my heart when I asked Jesus, "May I ask You a question, please?"

I never will forget it. When I said that, He turned around, walked three or four steps right back to where I was, and said, "Yes, you may."

I started, "Well, I've got two sermons from Mark chapter 5 that I preach in every revival meeting" (you see, I learned that from Jesus back in 1950 when He told me in a vision that He preached from the same text in Isaiah every time He went to a new place to minister).

I continued, "Both of these sermons came to me by inspiration."

NOT ALL SERMONS COME BY INSPIRATION

You see, the Apostle Paul told Timothy, a young minister, *"STUDY to shew thyself approved unto God, a workman that needeth not to be ashamed, rightly dividing the word of truth"* (2 Tim. 2:15).

Now I studied, all right. Sometimes just a text would be impressed on my heart, and I would start studying it and work up a message. Or a certain subject or title of a message would be on my heart, so I would start studying to develop the message. The full message would come over a period of time, sometimes after several days of working on it.

But these two messages from Mark 5 just came to me in an instant by the Spirit of God. They came by the inspiration of the moment.

Now one of the messages came just the week before the Lord appeared to me back in 1950. I was driving to Rockwall, Texas, from Garland, about ten miles, praying and singing in other tongues, and the Lord just dropped a message down inside my spirit.

When He did, I pulled off the highway onto the shoulder of the road. I got some notepaper out of my Bible, and I wrote down the outline. There were four points: a *destitute condition*, a *good report*, a *desperate act*, and a *glorious sequence*.

I was more of a sermonizer and a preacher in those days than I was a teacher, even though I did teach. Well, that was a good outline to preach from, wasn't it!

I had been meditating on the woman with the issue of blood. Number one, she was in a desperate condition. How much more desperate could you be than that woman? She'd had an issue of blood for twelve years and had suffered many things of many physicians. She'd spent all of her living; all her money was gone. Yet she was nothing bettered but rather grew worse. Isn't that a destitute condition?

But then, wait a minute—along came a good report about Jesus! She'd heard of Jesus. And when she did, she came in the press behind Him and touched His garment. That was her desperate act. So numbers two and three respectively were a good report and a desperate act.

And number four, there was a glorious sequence: She was healed and made whole! Jesus said, *"Daughter, thy faith hath made thee whole"* (Mark 5:34).

That's good preaching material! So I preached it that night. Then I began preaching that everywhere I went. In one of the services during each meeting I held, I'd preach those four points.

That happened in 1950. Then in late February and early March 1952, I was down in Alabama holding a meeting in a small church. I had planned to preach that same sermon. I'd improved on it some, because the more you preach something, the more light you'll get on it.

I had my notes on the pulpit and had my Bible opened to Mark chapter 5. I'd already read my text, and I began preaching this sermon that I'd received by inspiration. (When you get a sermon by inspiration, it'll last—you can just keep on preaching it. But when you just "work up" one, it might not last.)

Then I remember I looked down at my Bible, getting ready to expound on the first point when I noticed the words in Mark 5:28, "*FOR SHE SAID.*" I'd read them many times before. In fact, I'd just read them that night when I was in my room studying. But this time, those words "For she said" just sort of stood up on the page.

You might ask, "What do you mean, *they stood up on the page?*"

Well, you see, I didn't know everything about faith then that I know now. Sometimes it took me years to learn some things that I can teach you in two minutes. Some of my Rhema students and others who've heard me teach have thought, "Well, Brother Hagin always knew that."

I know about faith now, but I had to learn it just like you had to learn it or have to learn it. And when those words "For she said" stood out to me like that, I didn't know all about the "saying" part of faith like I do now.

Anyway, I looked down at that page in my Bible, and those words "For she said" looked like they were three times bigger than the rest of the words on the page. That's what I mean when I say they just sort of stood up on the page.

I saw something new that I hadn't seen before, and I just took off preaching on it. So that made two sermons from Mark 5 that I received instantly by the inspiration of the Holy Ghost.

So I said to Jesus in the vision I had there in the home of Brother and Sister Fisher, "I've received these two sermons from Mark chapter 5 by inspiration. I preach them everywhere I go. But, now, it seems to me at particular times in prayer when I'm waiting before God that there's another sermon or message in this passage that You're trying to get across to me that will complement those other two message. I could be wrong, but it seems to me You're trying to get that other message over to my spirit."

Someone might ask, "Why didn't that third sermon just come by inspiration like the other two did?" I don't know. I don't know everything, but the matter had been on my heart, so I asked Jesus about it that night.

And so Jesus said, "You're right. I have been trying to get that over to you. Get your pencil and paper, and I'll give it to you."

When Jesus said, "Get your pencil and paper, and I'll give it to you," I opened my eyes and got up off my knees from where I had been kneeling in front of a chair. I said to one of the ladies who was there with us, "In my bedroom, on the table by the bed, you'll find a pencil and a notepad. Please get it for me."

I always kept a pencil and pad by my bed, because many times as I'd pray in the nighttime, the Lord would give me something, and I'd write it down. If you don't write down what the Lord gives you, oftentimes, you'll forget it.

The lady I asked to get my pencil and paper came back with them and handed them to me. We'd all been just sitting there, praising God. Then I closed my eyes again, and I saw Jesus standing there—He was just as real to me as the people in that living room were when I had my eyes open. And Jesus picked up His conversation right where He left off when He'd said, "Go get your pencil and paper."

Jesus said to me, "Write down *one, two, three, four,*" so I knew the message would have four points (I actually still have the original piece of paper that I wrote this on when Jesus first gave it to me!).

I wrote down one, two, three, four, just as the Lord had said. I never opened my eyes, and it was surprising how well and straight I wrote with my eyes shut! I skipped spaces between each number because I knew there would be some information to go with each point.

'HOW TO WRITE YOUR OWN TICKET'

The Lord was giving me another message from Mark chapter 5 about the woman with the issue of blood. I won't give the whole message, but I want to give you something that fits in with healing and the healing anointing. (I included the complete message in my minibook *How To Write Your Own Ticket With God.*)

Jesus gave me the four points. Then He said, "If anybody anywhere will take these four steps or put these four principles into operation, he will always receive whatever he wants from Me or from God the Father."

Well, if what Jesus said is true (and it is), everybody ought to get hold of it and do it, because it won't work for you just because you *know* it. You'll have to *act* on it for it to work for you. Not acting on what you know would be like somebody saying, "Well, I don't understand. I just don't understand what's wrong. You know, I've got a telephone right there on the table by my bed, but it never works."

Why doesn't it work? Because the person doesn't work it! That telephone won't ever work unless he works it. I mean, even if it rings, he still has to do something. He still has to pick up the receiver and say, "Hello."

Jesus said to me in that vision, "If anyone anywhere will take these four steps or put these four principles into operation, he will always receive whatever he wants from Me or from God the Father." Well, that "anyone" is *you!* Wherever you're from, these steps or principles apply to *you.*

You Can Have What You Say

Now Jesus didn't explain that statement to me: "If anyone anywhere will *take these four steps* or *put these four principles into operation . . . .*" He didn't have to; I understood exactly what He meant by it.

You see, there are some things that are yours right now, such as salvation, the baptism in the Holy Ghost, divine healing, finances, and spiritual victory. And anything that the Bible *promises* you now, you can *receive* now by taking the four *steps* Jesus gave to me in the vision.

There are other things that take more time to develop, such as some financial needs and the manifestation of some healings. In that case, the four *steps* become four *principles* that you have to abide by over a period of time until what you want comes to pass.

So for the things that are already yours now, you can take what Jesus showed me as *steps* to receive them. For other things, you can take what He showed me as *principles* to abide by over a period of time to receive those things, because it takes time for them to come to pass.

But, thank God, whether they are steps to be taken immediately or principles to be practiced over time, *you can have what you say*!

Jesus said, "Anyone who will take these four steps or put these four principles into operation will *always* receive . . . ." How many times will they receive? A few times? No, they will *always* receive an answer.

So I took my cue from what He said and called my sermon "How To Write Your Own Ticket With God."

Number one, Jesus said, "*Say it.*"

Number two, He said, "*Do it.*"

Number three, He said, "*Receive it.*"

Number four, Jesus said, "*Tell it.*"

These four points came from Mark 5:27–34 concerning the woman with the issue of blood. Verses 27 and 28 say, "*When she had heard of Jesus, came in the press behind, and touched his garment. FOR SHE SAID, If I may touch but his clothes, I shall be whole.*"

You see, first, she *said* it: "If I may touch but His clothes, I shall be whole."

Then she *did* it. She "came in the press behind and touched His garment."

Then she *received* it: "*And straightway the fountain of her blood was dried up; and she felt in her body that she was healed of that plague*" (v. 29).

Then she *told* it: "*The woman fearing and trembling, knowing what was done in her, came and fell down before him, and told him all the truth*" (v. 33).

And Jesus said to her, "*Daughter, thy faith hath made thee whole; go in peace, and be whole of thy plague*" (v. 34).

Isn't that simple? Yet Jesus never did give anything complex. Did you ever stop to think about the fact that as Jesus preached to folks when He was on the earth, He talked about sheep, sheepfolds, shepherds, grapes, vineyards, and so forth? He taught so the people could understand Him.

You wouldn't believe it today to hear me preach or teach, but in my early days of ministry, I used big words and theological terms that a lot of people didn't understand.

I started out as a preacher in another denomination. Then even after I received the baptism in the Holy Ghost and came over into Pentecostal circles, I was cold and stiff in my preaching many times. My wife said to me once, "I believe you could preach standing in a wash pan." You see, I never moved from behind the pulpit when I preached! I just stood there, straight as a string and stiff as a board! I would stand there behind the pulpit, "just *so.*"

I was trained to preach that way. And I studied big words in preparing my sermons.

My wife would never criticize me. She's only said a couple things to me in my more than sixty years in ministry. And even then, it was what you'd call good criticism, not destructive criticism.

But my wife did say something to me about using big words in my sermons. She said, "Honey, why do you use all those big words when you preach? Nobody understands them, and you have to take fifteen minutes just to explain what the words mean."

JESUS TOLD ME TO KEEP IT SIMPLE

My wife didn't know it, but the Lord used her, because He'd already been dealing with me about that very thing. The Lord kept saying to me, "Keep it simple. Keep it simple. Keep it simple."

You see, when I received the baptism in the Holy Ghost, the Holy Ghost began to talk to me in a more real way. And one day the Lord through the Spirit said to me, "The people I preached to had very little or no education. The masses of people had no education. And I got right down on the level where they were."

That's the reason I started way back in 1939 just trying to say things the simplest way I could say them—the simplest and the plainest way. I endeavored to keep it simple.

Jesus said to me, "I talked in terms the people could understand. I talked about shepherds, sheepfolds, vineyards, grapes, and so forth, so they could understand what I was saying." Then He repeated to me, "Keep it simple."

So I began to obey the Spirit of God.

You see, He never did give anybody anything that was so complex that he couldn't understand. What good would it be for the Lord to give you something if it were complex and you couldn't understand it? He'd be wasting His time. And you know God is not stupid; He's not going to waste His time.

So the Lord gave me these four simple little ole steps: *Say* it; *do* it; *receive* it; *tell* it.

WHAT JESUS SHOWED ME APPLIES TO THE HEALING ANOINTING

Now the part I want to emphasize is step three, the *receiving* part.

You see, Jesus gave me these four points from Mark 5, the story of the woman with the issue of blood. She *said* it; *did* it; *received* it; and *told* it.

Well, we know from reading from this passage that it said, *"Jesus, immediately knowing in himself that VIRTUE* [power] *HAD GONE OUT OF HIM, turned him about in the press, and said, Who touched my clothes?"* (Mark 5:30). Jesus was ministering with the healing anointing. It was the healing anointing that went out of Jesus and into the woman with the issue of blood and healed her.

But notice something. She had to *receive* it. Jesus couldn't receive it for her. He could minister with the healing anointing, but He could not receive it for her. *She* received it.

How do you receive the healing anointing? *By faith.*

That agrees exactly with the principles of faith that are revealed and given to us elsewhere throughout the Bible. Mark 11:24 is one example: *"Therefore I say unto you, What things soever ye desire, when ye pray, believe that ye receive them, and ye shall have them."*

The principle of faith in Mark 11:24, "believe you receive them and you shall have them," is the same principle in Mark 5. You've got to receive whatever it is you need or want. And you receive it by faith.

FAITH RECEIVES FROM GOD WHETHER OR NOT THE ANOINTING IS PRESENT

In connection with the healing anointing, we know that one can be anointed with this power. Yet, right on the other hand, Jesus said to me, "Power is always present everywhere."

You see, folks think, "If I could just get Brother Hagin or somebody else who's anointed to lay hands on me, I could be healed." Well, that may be so, all right, but it isn't necessary.

Now notice, God anointed Jesus with the healing power. Yet in all of God's fullness, His power is always present everywhere. We can't totally comprehend that with our little ole peanut brains, but it's so nonetheless!

Is God any less powerful wherever you are? No!

By way of illustration, we have some beautiful musicians at our ministry. Some of them play at Healing School every day. Others play during crusades and on-the-road meetings. And others play at the church every Sunday and Wednesday.

Let me ask you a question. If all of those musicians were to travel out of town—say, from Tulsa to Oklahoma City—would they be any less accomplished or good at what they do? No, because the same attributes and capabilities they possess here in Tulsa, they still possess no matter where they go.

Jesus said to me, "God is always present everywhere with all of His attributes and capabilities." Well, since God with all of His attributes and capabilities is always present everywhere, then all of His *power* is always present everywhere too.

The difference between the *healing anointing that one can be anointed with* and the *healing power of God that's always present everywhere* is this: With the power of God that is always present everywhere, it takes a little bit more faith on your part to receive it.

You see, back down on this lesser level, you could hear somebody preach who's anointed with the healing power of God. You could believe that he's anointed, and you could receive the healing power that he's anointed with and receive your healing. That's the reason God anoints people to minister His healing power to others. He wants to get right down to where people are in their faith.

Yet right on the other hand, power is always present everywhere because *God* is always present everywhere. And you could receive that power by faith.

"Well, now," somebody said, "if that power's there, why doesn't it just work?"

I like to give the testimony of my own healing to explain the answer to that question. I was bedfast for sixteen months. Actually, I was sick for approximately the first seventeen years of my life. I never ran and played like other little children. I became totally bedfast at age fifteen with two serious organic heart troubles—a deformed heart and an incurable blood disease. Eventually, I was totally paralyzed and had wasted away till I weighed only eighty-nine pounds.

And yet on the eighth day of August 1934 at about ten o'clock in the morning, after being bedfast for sixteen months, I was healed!

To be honest, after I acted upon what I knew the Bible said in Mark 11:24, I didn't feel anything to begin with. But then the Spirit within me said, "Now you believe you're well."

I said, "I sure do."

He said, "Get up then. Well people ought to be up at this time in the morning." And ordinarily, that would be the case. Well people *would* be up at ten o'clock in the morning.

When the Lord said that, the thought crossed my mind, "How am I going to get up? I'm paralyzed."

But *when I made the effort,* I felt the power of God! I didn't really know how the power of God felt. I'd never felt it like that before in my life. I'd sensed His Presence, and I knew that the Holy Ghost was in me, bearing witness with my spirit that I was a child of God (Rom. 8:16). But I'd never felt the power of God like that before.

I felt something come down over me and sort of strike me in the top of my head. It traveled down over my head and shoulders, down my body, down my limbs, out the end of my fingers, then down my entire body and out the end of my toes. It was like a warm glow, and when it went out the end of my toes, I was standing just as straight, healed, and whole as I am today. All the paralysis was gone, and my body was completely healed!

Now what caused that to happen? That power didn't just come that day. The power that healed me was in my room all of those sixteen months I was bedfast. Then why didn't it work?

You see, that's where we've missed it. We thought if the power was there, it's just going to do the job. But that's simply not true. *Faith* must be mixed with the power for it to work.

I use the illustration that in the same bedroom where I was healed and raised up from the deathbed, over behind the bed was an electrical outlet—a receptacle—in the wall.

Well, during the entire sixteen months I lay sick in that bedroom, nothing was ever plugged into that outlet. You couldn't say the power wasn't there. I couldn't have said, "Don't plug anything into that outlet; there's no power there."

No, at any time, somebody could have plugged a light into that outlet, and that light would have burned. In the wintertime, somebody could have plugged an electric heater in there, and we would have had heat. And in the summertime, somebody could have plugged a fan into that outlet, and the fan would have worked.

But during that entire sixteen months, nobody ever used that outlet behind the bed. So in one sense, it never worked.

Well, did it not work because the power wasn't there? No, the power was there. At any time, somebody could have decided to use that outlet, and it would have worked. But nobody ever plugged anything in to it. Nobody ever plugged into the power!

It's the same way with the power of God. It's a simple thought, yet it's stupendous. God's power is always present everywhere. Whether you're specially anointed or not, the power of God is there! And *faith* plugs into it!

Jesus said to me, "Faith puts the power to work." In other words, faith *uses* the power; faith *activates* it.

Jesus was anointed with that same power that's always present everywhere—the power of God. The reason He was anointed with it is that God had to have some way to come down and reach people through their physical senses. They were too natural; there was no other way to get to them.

God had to do that then by anointing Jesus, and He has to do that now by anointing others. There's no other way to get to some people.

When Jesus ministered on the earth, the people could *see* Jesus. They could *hear* Him talk. And that's the reason God has anointed me and others. People can see us, hear us, feel our hands as we lay them on their foreheads for prayer. It's a lower level of faith. Yet it works, thank God!

However, the same principle works whether someone who's anointed lays hands on you or whether you believe God on your own like I did. Power is always present everywhere. And *faith* activates it.

We see that in the case of the woman with the issue of blood. The power that Jesus was anointed with flowed out to her because her faith made a demand on the power. Yet that power didn't flow out to the whole multitude, because Jesus said, "*Somebody touched Me. Who touched Me?*" His disciples said, "*Thou seest the multitude thronging thee, and sayest thou, Who touched me?*" (Mark 5:31).

A whole multitude of people was present, yet that power didn't flow out to the whole multitude; it just flowed out to the woman with the issue of blood. Why? Her faith activated the power that Jesus was anointed with.

A DOORKNOB OR A LIVE WIRE?

Again and again, I've seen folks *not* mixing their faith with the healing power. I've laid hands on people with the anointing in manifestation, and it was like laying my hands on a doorknob. I mean, there was no response! It just felt dead. I knew those people weren't in faith and that they wouldn't receive anything, but I didn't tell them.

I know a lot of things about people that I don't tell them. And I don't just imagine it; I know it by the Spirit of God. But most of the time I don't tell them, because it just wouldn't be wise to do that. It's not wise to tell people everything you know. Many times they'll get mad and won't come back to a meeting. But if you can keep them coming, and the Word gets into them, then faith will come.

I've had those same people who didn't respond in faith to the anointing come back and receive their healing after four, five, six, or seven times—some of them came to be prayed for as many as seventeen or eighteen times!

Someone said, "You laid hands on them eighteen times?" Yes, and each of the first seventeen times, there was not a thing in the world in the way of a response. It was like I'd laid my hands on a doorknob or a stick of wood. In fact, when I'd see them coming, I'd think, "Oh, dear God, here they come again." Well, if they had still been like they were in their faith, they wouldn't have gotten anything.

Those folks would come back in the healing line, and I'd think, "I'll just hurry up and lay hands on them. They're not going to get anything anyway." And if they had been like they were, they *wouldn't* have gotten anything. But I didn't want to hurt their feelings, so I would just hurry and lay hands on them. Besides, if I could keep them coming back, after a while, they might get something. Their faith might get developed so they could receive.

Many times when I've laid hands on people after they'd been in the healing line several times, it felt like I'd gotten hold of a live wire! When I'd laid hands on them before, it was dead; there was no response. But when they responded in faith, the healing anointing was activated. They shook, I shook, and they fell over backward under the mighty power of God! Many times the anointing was so strong that I'd fall over too. I didn't know that was going to happen. Sometimes it startled me—the power was that strong.

What happened? Somewhere along the line, their faith began working, and their faith activated that power or anointing.

So then, we can conclude that the healing power of God is passive, inert, or dormant until faith is exercised. Even though it's present, it has to be activated by faith.

RECEIVING THE ANOINTING IS NOT LIMITED TO THE LAYING ON OF HANDS

The power of God is always present everywhere. You don't even have to have hands laid on you. But, of course, if that's your level of faith, then you'll have to release the healing power of God on your behalf through the laying on of hands. But either way, *you* have to *receive* the healing!

On the other hand, no one has to have hands laid on him to be healed of anything. He can receive it himself by faith in God's Word, because power is always present everywhere.

I remember one time there was a lady who came to Healing School. Actually, she stopped here in Tulsa on her way to the great Mayo Clinic in Rochester, Minnesota. Doctors had sent her to the clinic along with all her medical records. She'd been operated on six months before, and the surgeon accidentally slit her esophagus, so she couldn't swallow. She hadn't swallowed in six months and had lost about ninety pounds.

I saw her sitting in the back of the auditorium in Healing School. She had a tube in her nose, and she had to be fed liquids through that tube. She couldn't eat.

We later learned that her neck was a solid mass of scars. Doctors had made eleven different incisions, trying to correct her problem. So they sent her to the Mayo Clinic to see what they could do about it.

I never did lay hands on that woman or pray for her. The Spirit of God was in manifestation that day (whether He is in manifestation or not, He is present; and if you start believing that, He'll come into manifestation!). I said to the crowd, "He's here, praise God. Just reach up and take your healing."

Later this woman testified that when I said that, she said, "Well, I'll just receive healing myself right now. That's it, glory to God, I receive my healing." Then she just reached up and pulled the tube out of her nose.

The Healing School meeting ended. This woman hadn't had a solid bite of food in six months. She went across the street to what was then a Mexican restaurant and ate two Mexican dinners! She was healed! And she testified a couple of days later.

Boy, when you haven't had a solid bite of food in your stomach for six months, you're bound to be healed if you can eat two Mexican dinners!

Well, what activated the healing power in that woman to heal her body? The power was present that day as it always is. We just happened to sense the manifestation of it a little more at that particular time. As a matter of fact, as I looked across the crowd that day, it looked almost like a fog had come into the room, and it hung over the people's heads. That's a physical manifestation. You also see that happening throughout the Old Testament. A cloud would appear, and that cloud was a manifestation of the glory or power of God.

What is the glory of God? It's the Spirit of God. That's what the Bible said. The Bible said that Jesus was raised up from the dead by the glory of the Father (Rom. 6:4). Then two chapters later, it said the *Spirit* raised Jesus up (Rom. 8:11). So we know the glory of God is the Spirit of God. And His power is everywhere present at all times to bless, heal, deliver, and meet your need.

You could receive your healing right now just like that woman did in Healing School and just like the woman with the issue of blood did in Mark chapter 5. You can write your own ticket with God by faith. Faith *receives*. Faith activates the power of God!

---

[1]For a further study on this subject, see Rev. Hagin's books *I Believe in Visions* and *The Ministry Gifts.*

—Chapter 5—

RECEIVING HEALING THROUGH THE ANOINTED WORD

And it shall come to pass in that day, that his burden shall be taken away from off thy shoulder, and his yoke from off thy neck, and the yoke shall be destroyed because of the anointing.

—Isaiah 10:27

We talked about the healing anointing that's available today to heal sick bodies. We also learned how to tap into that healing flow by faith. But here's something else we need to realize in connection with healing and the healing anointing. You can actually receive the same results through faith without the tangible anointing.

You need to realize that. *You can receive the same results through faith without the anointing!*

I started preaching at age seventeen when I was healed in 1934 as a young Baptist boy. I wasn't conscious of any anointing in my ministry. It was after I was baptized in the Holy Ghost in 1937 that I became conscious at times of the anointing. Then after that in September 1950, the Lord appeared to me in a vision and said, "I've given thee a special anointing to minister to the sick."

But during my first years of ministry, if I ever felt any anointing to minister to the sick, I didn't know it (and if you were anointed with the healing anointing, you'd know it, because it's a tangible substance!).

But during those first years in the ministry, I'd simply teach people what the Bible said and then say, "I'm going to lay my hands on you now, because the Bible said, 'These signs shall follow them that believe . . .'" (Mark 16:17–18).

I didn't feel anything *before* I laid hands on those people; I didn't feel anything *when* I laid hands on them; and I didn't feel anything *after* I laid hands on them. Most of the time I just felt dry! As we say down in Texas, "dry as a shuck"! That's how I felt. Yet people would get healed right and left, coming and going.

After I was baptized in the Holy Ghost and spoke with other tongues, I came over among the Pentecostals. I talked to neighboring pastors who were Pentecostal, and I found out that before I received the baptism of the Holy Ghost, about five times as many people were healed under my ministry as were under any one of their ministries.

I got more people healed *before* I received the baptism in the Holy Ghost than any five Pentecostal preachers! Why? Because I taught people faith, and, together, we believed God. Most of the Pentecostal preachers didn't do any teaching on faith, or they did very little at all. They would just wait for the anointing, which did manifest at times.

BASE YOUR FAITH ON THE WORD, NOT ON THE ANOINTING

Modern-day Charismatics don't know much about it, but in the days of *The Voice of Healing*, there was a healing revival here in America from 1947 through 1958. There were many great preachers who were anointed to minister healing by the anointing.

Ministers put tents up everywhere. One preacher had a tent that would seat 20,000. Another minister finally had a tent that would seat 22,000. And any number of preachers had tents that would seat 5,000 or 10,000. Tents were just popping up every-where because of this healing revival.

Most of those preachers ministered with the healing anointing, but they knew very little about just believing God and His Word. Well, thank God for the anointing, but if you don't get your faith working and get your ministry founded on the basis of the Word, your ministry and your effectiveness won't last too long.

I was in one preacher's meeting during this revival of healing. There was a good anointing in the service to preach and teach, but the anointing to minister healing just wasn't there.

Several of us ministers were sitting on the platform. When the preacher finished his sermon, he gave an altar call, and there must have been a hundred people respond to be saved. That was a large crowd in those days. We don't think it's such a big thing if a hun-dred people answer an altar call today. But in those days, that was phenomenal.

It was advertised that this minister was also supposed to minis-ter to the sick. But after the altar call that evening, he turned to us on the platform and said, "Boy, you couldn't pray for the sick in an atmosphere like *this!*"

You see, he sensed that the healing anointing he usually ministered under was not present. Now don't misunderstand me. The Spirit of God, the anointing, was there. The Spirit of God had led those hundred people to come to the altar to get saved. But I'm talking about the *healing* anointing now. There is a difference, and I'll explain it in more detail in another chapter.

So this minister just sort of passed or skipped by laying hands on the sick, even though he had been laying hands on the sick every night in the services.

One minister sitting by me said, "I don't understand that; the power of God is here. Why can't He minister healing?"

But I understood it. The anointing that he usually ministered under just wasn't in manifestation, so he didn't know what to do. He didn't know how to minister by simple faith in God and His Word.

THE DIFFERENCE BETWEEN THE HEALING POWER AND SIMPLE FAITH IN THE WORD

In this chapter, I'm going to explain the difference between *ministering* healing by the healing anointing and ministering healing by faith in the Word through the laying on of hands. And I'm also going to explain the difference between *receiving* healing by faith mixed with the anointing and receiving healing by simple faith in the anointed Word.

In my own ministry, I minister under the same healing anointing with which that preacher ministered under during the days of *The Voice of Healing.* I minister with the healing anointing at times as the Spirit wills, just like he did. But this preacher didn't minister to the sick that particular night because the healing anointing wasn't present. And as I said, he just didn't know what to do.

After that minister's meeting, I was holding a service in my own meeting, and boy, was it dry! It was a church meeting because I mainly held church meetings instead of tent meetings. The Lord had spoken to me very definitely and said, "Stay in the churches." (When God told me to change courses and do something differently, I did it differently. I always obeyed His instructions.)

So I was in the churches, and I had been running long meetings, holding services every night for three to nine weeks in one church, and sometimes twice a day Monday through Friday.

I'd hold these meetings, and sometimes as a result of a particular meeting, the Sunday school attendance would double or triple in the church. The church membership would double. I remember in one church, the pastor had twelve times as many men in his church when I left as he did when I first got there. Our results were just overwhelming. But, you see, God said to go to the churches, so that's what I did.

Well, this particular service I was in was dull and dry. We'd been running the meeting for two or three weeks already. Because the people were staying up late every night, after a while, they got tired. We'd been having a good meeting, with people getting saved and baptized with the Holy Ghost. But in this particular service, it was just dull and dry.

It wasn't the devil making the service dry; it was the flesh. The weather was cool, and many of the folks in the church would work hard, go home, and then eat a big supper before coming to sit down in that warm church building. And they'd grow sleepy. So after two or three weeks of services, it wasn't the devil who was making the service dry. It was just a matter of the flesh.

LEARN TO RECOGNIZE THE ENEMY OF FAITH

The devil said to my mind, "If I were you, I'd hurry and dismiss the people and send them home early to get a good night's sleep. You can come back tomorrow and have a good service then. After all, as dull as this service is, you couldn't do anything tonight anyway."

Those were the thoughts that were going through my mind. I recognized that it was the devil putting those thoughts there. Anything that's doubt and unbelief is of the devil. That's easily discernible, isn't it?

Well, if I'm depending on the anointing alone to minister healing to folks, then I'm going to do just like the other preacher did. I'm just going to dismiss the crowd and send them home. I can't minister the tangible healing anointing when it's not there! And I'm not going to lie about it. If I don't have it, I don't have it.

I never felt so dull and dry spiritually in my life as I felt in that service. In fact, if I'd been going by the way I felt, I would have said, "Folks, before I give an altar call, I want everybody to pray for *me*—I feel backslidden"!

Have you ever felt that way? Have you ever felt like you didn't have anything to give—like you were dry, empty, listless, and powerless?

Why, certainly, every one of us has felt that way at one time or another in life. In a meeting once, I mentioned the fact that all of us feel dry at some time or another, and someone came up to me afterwards, just amazed. He asked, "Brother Hagin, you mean preachers are that way too?"

I said, "Yes, preachers are that way too. They're just as human as you are. They have the devil, the flesh, and the world to deal with, just like you do."

So I would have closed out that meeting for the night, but, you see, I knew something about faith! I knew that feelings didn't have a thing in the world to do with faith. I knew that what I felt or didn't feel—whether I felt the anointing or not—didn't have a thing in the world to do with faith!

Thoughts of just sending everyone home for the night were coming to my mind as fast as machine-gun bullets can fly: "Why don't you just dismiss the service and send them home? Nobody could get anything from God in an atmosphere like this. It's too dead and dry, and everybody's nearly asleep. Let them get a good night's sleep, and they'll come back refreshed tomorrow night. Then maybe they'll get something from the service."

I recognized those thoughts as coming from the devil, so I just acted like he wasn't saying a thing; I ignored him. I closed my sermon and said to the crowd, "I'll tell you what I'm going to do. I'm going to lay my hands on the first person who comes down here to the altar for healing, and that person will be healed. And the first person down here who doesn't have the baptism of the Holy Ghost, I'm going to lay my hands on him or her to be baptized with the Holy Ghost, and he or she will receive. So who's it going to be?"

I wasn't what you'd call *inspired* to say that! Sometimes you do get inspired to say things like that, and it's hard when you're not! But I just deliberately made myself say it because I knew what the Word said. It seemed like what I did was *me* entirely— like it was me doing it myself with no help from God at all. I just put myself out on a limb, so to speak.

FAITH IS MOVED BY THE WORD, NOT BY FEELINGS

Well, when I said that to the crowd, everybody just sat there. I mean, *nobody moved*! It seemed like ten minutes, but, you know, ten *seconds* can seem like ten minutes when a service is as dead and dry as this one was!

Finally, a dear lady got up from her seat. A few people in the crowd woke up and sort of blinked their eyes. This lady said, "Well, I've been seeking the baptism in the Holy Ghost for years. Do you reckon I might get it tonight?"

I said, "There's no might or maybe about it. Come down here. I'll lay hands on you, and you'll be filled with the Holy Ghost!"

So she came down to the altar. I laid hands on her, and she started talking in tongues!

After that, a few people got excited. But this was a Pentecostal church, you see. And about half the crowd were saying to themselves in effect, "Well now, he's teaching that you can get the Holy Ghost without tarrying for it. That's not real; she didn't get the real thing like we did. We had to tarry."

I could sense that. I could feel the division in the crowd. A few people—about ten to twelve—were rejoicing over this woman's receiving the baptism in the Holy Ghost. But there was division in the congregation.

So I just quickly repeated my first invitation: "I'll lay my hands on the first one down here for healing, and you'll be healed."

The congregation just sat there and looked at me. Finally, a dear fellow started trying to get up. He had a homemade crutch under one arm and what looked like a crooked little tree limb in his other hand. He finally made it up out of his seat and came toward the altar.

I thought, "Dear God, surely somebody could have come who had a chronic headache!" But this fellow came instead. It seemed like it took him forever to get to the altar. Everybody just sat and watched.

Well, what are you going to do in a situation like that? You've got to fight your flesh and feelings!

I *felt* like turning and running. I would have fallen through a crack in the platform, but there wasn't any big enough to hide me!

What are you going to do, though, if you've already given the invitation? You're going to act like it's so! You're going to just grin and wait for the person to get there because God's Word is true!

All the time this fellow was making his way to the front, thoughts were running through my mind: "Boy, he's going to show you up now. That poor fellow isn't going to get a thing, and they're all going to think this faith business doesn't work."

What did I do? First, I recognized that it was the devil who was talking to me, and I just ignored him. I didn't pay any attention to him.

You see, when you're in faith, you're not moved. On the inside, you say, "I'm not moved by what I see."

That poor fellow was gnarled and crippled, just limping down the aisle with a homemade crutch in one hand and a stick in the other one! But I wasn't moved by what I saw. I wasn't moved by what I felt (when you're in faith, you don't have to feel a thing).

I'm not moved by what I feel or see. I'm moved only by what I believe!

That crippled man finally made it down the aisle to the front of the church. I laid hands on him and, bless God, his crutch fell one way and his stick fell the other way. His body straightened up, and he started jumping around in front of the whole church!

And do you know what? That whole place got lively! I mean, they were jumping, hollering, shouting, and praising God from the front of the sanctuary to the back. It may have been dull and dry in that service before, but we *all* felt something then! Why? Because the power of God was released! The power or the anointing was released through faith, and that power healed the crippled man and drove the devil out of his body!

Thank God for the anointing! I love the anointing, but if I don't have it upon me, I'm going to go right ahead and tell people what the Bible said and lay hands on them according to the Word.

THERE'S POWER TO HEAL IN THE ANOINTED WORD!

Do you remember on one occasion it said in the Gospels that Jesus cast out the spirits with His Word (Matt. 8:16)? Well, when the tangible anointing is not present, I'm just going to go ahead and say the Word. What is it? It's the Word of faith!

The Bible also said in the Gospels concerning the ministry of Jesus that He *"went about all the cities and villages, TEACHING in their synagogues, and PREACHING the gospel of the kingdom, and HEALING every sickness and every disease among the people"* (Matt. 9:35). Jesus was anointed to do all three of those things— *teach, preach,* and *heal.*

That scripture, Matthew 9:35, is talking about the healing anointing when it says Jesus went about *"healing every sickness and every disease among the people."*

If God has specially anointed you, you can minister healing, too, under the anointing. But you can also get the same results without any anointing, just by faith in God's Word. We have God's Word for it: *". . . they shall lay hands on the sick, and they shall recover"* (Mark 16:18).

That's one way a person can receive healing—just by acting in faith on the Word. For instance, I was healed and raised up from a deathbed years ago just through faith in God's Word— through acting upon the promises of God, Mark 11:23 and 24, for myself.

MARK 11:23-24

23 For verily I say unto you, That whosoever shall say unto this mountain, Be thou removed, and be thou cast into the sea; and shall not doubt in his heart, but shall believe that those things which he saith shall come to pass; he shall have whatsoever he saith.

24 Therefore I say unto you, What things soever ye desire, when ye pray, believe that ye receive them, and ye shall have them.

I've seen many people healed through acting in faith on the Word. I've prayed for people who were given up by medical science to die. The best doctors in the world had done their best; there just wasn't anything in the natural that could be done.

I prayed once for a certain woman who had been given up to die. I never felt a thing in the world when I prayed, and she never felt a thing in the world. We just prayed according to the Word of God, and within two days she was perfectly well!

Now right at the moment I prayed, the woman didn't seem any better. But the next day she was considerably better. And the following day, she was a hundred percent all right!

She went right back to the same doctors who'd said nothing more could be done. The doctors couldn't find a trace of the disease! It was completely gone!

That happened without the healing anointing in manifestation. That woman was healed as a result of simple faith in the anointed Word!

You can receive the same results through faith in the anointed Word as you can by receiving healing through the healing anointing!

EXAMPLES OF THE POWER OF FAITH IN GOD'S WORD

To further illustrate this point, I want to share with you another example along this same line. A young man came to our Healing School years ago. His mother was Presbyterian, but she had received the baptism in the Holy Ghost and had gotten into the Charismatic movement. Afterward, she tried to talk to her son about the Lord, but he was involved in the hippie movement, and, really, they had no communication.

Then her son went back to college at the age of twenty-seven, deciding that he was going to be a lawyer. He'd had some kind of a little growth on one of his limbs, and the growth suddenly flared up. He thought nothing of it for a while, but it got worse, so he went to the doctor.

His doctor sent him to a cancer specialist. The specialist took a biopsy of the growth and told the young man it was the very worst kind of cancer. The doctors wanted to take his limb off immediately.

"No," he said, "I'm not going to let you do it."

They said, "If we don't, you'll be dead in thirty days."

"Well," the young man asked, "what are my chances of living if you *do* take the limb off?"

They told him that after removing the limb and giving him treatments, he had a fifty-fifty chance.

"No," the young man said, "I'm not going to do it."

So this young man went to another cancer clinic. He didn't tell the doctors there that he'd been anywhere else. They ran their tests and said the same thing: "You have cancer—the very worst kind. We need to take your limb off immediately."

"No," he said, "I'm not going to let you do it."

They said, "You'll be dead in thirty days."

The young man wasn't satisfied with that, so he went to a third cancer clinic. Doctors there said the same thing—that he'd be dead in thirty days.

The young man called his mother, and his mother said, "Brother Hagin just started a healing school in Tulsa. Let's go there." This young man was not a Christian, but he agreed to come to Healing School with his mother.

At Healing School, we prayed for people under the healing anointing. The power of God would go into them, and they'd fall on the floor under the power of God. Well, this young man didn't understand that; he'd never been around the anointing. He'd never been around any kind of church or church group, much less our kind! So when he saw people falling on the floor under the power of God, he said to his mother, "I don't understand that."

I taught Healing School in those days, and in the process of teaching on healing, I always worked my own testimony in somewhere. So I gave my testimony of how I was healed of a deformed heart and an incurable blood disease just by acting on God's Word, Mark 11:23 and 24.

This young man said to his mother, "I see that; I can understand that." So he sat right there in his seat in Healing School and said, "I just believe I receive my healing." He later said he didn't feel a thing when he said that. He simply believed he received his healing.

You see, feelings have nothing to do with believing God's Word. "Well, how do you feel?" someone might ask a person who's just believed he received his healing.

"I don't feel any different, but the *Bible* said . . . ."

Do you see that feelings have nothing to do with simply believing what the Bible said? *Faith believes whether it feels anything or not.*

Well, this young man believed what the Bible said.

What happened to him? Well, he was healed through his faith in the anointed Word, and years later he's still alive and well! He went back to one of the same clinics where he was diagnosed, and they couldn't find a trace of cancer. It all disappeared. Hallelujah!

Here was this young man, sitting in Healing School, not even saved. He never felt a thing: He just believed he received his healing, and he was healed. Eight months later, he went for final tests at the cancer clinic, and one of the doctors said, "Just don't come back anymore. The cancer's gone. That's it. Forget about coming back."

The young man called his mother to give the good report. He said, "Jesus healed me." His mother answered, "Son, don't ever forget that Jesus is your Healer."

When she said that, his voice broke and he said, "Yes, and He's my Savior too." He knew Jesus had healed him, and he was acquainted with Jesus as his Healer. But somewhere along the line, he became acquainted with Jesus as his Savior too!

How did that young man receive healing? Was it by the healing anointing? No, it was by faith in God's Word.

FAITH MOVES THE HAND OF GOD!

Along the same line, one lady asked me to pray for her aunt who was the black sheep of their family. You know, nearly everybody's got a black sheep in his or her family. Do you know what I mean by "black sheep"? One dictionary defines it as *a discreditable member of a respectable group.*

This lady said she had tried to talk to her aunt. Her aunt drank and was an alcoholic. She smoked and had been a prostitute a good part of her life. She just lived a very immoral, mean, ugly life. She was full of evil. Every time this lady tried to talk to her aunt about the Lord, her aunt "cussed her out."

Then, because she had some physical problems, the aunt went into the hospital for a routine checkup and tests. When the test results came back, the doctors told her, "Well, we've got some bad news."

"What is it?" she asked.

"You've got cancer," they said. "It's spread all over your body. You'll be dead in ten days."

Well, her niece said to me, "Brother Hagin, I'm going to see her. She may cuss me out, but I'm going anyway. I'm going to talk to her. You pray for me."

So she went to visit her aunt. At first, she talked to her aunt about the weather and so forth. Then she said to her, "Aunt _____, I've come to pray for you."

Her aunt began to cry and said, "Yeah, I want you to." So the niece prayed the sinner's prayer with her.

Afterward, her aunt said, "Thank God, I'm saved. I'm going to Heaven. I'm ready to die now."

The niece said, "But you don't have to die, not at your age." The woman was only in her late forties. She didn't know much about the Bible because she had just gotten saved. So her niece just read to her Mark 11:23 and 24.

"Is that really in the Bible?" her aunt asked. So the niece showed it to her and let her see it for herself.

"Why, it *is* in the Bible!" the aunt said. "You mean, all we have to do then is just pray and believe we receive, and we'll have it? That's it?"

"Yes. That's it," her niece replied.

"Well, just pray, and I'll believe!"

So her niece laid hands on her, and her aunt believed she received her healing. Then the aunt began to tell every one of the nurses, "You know, according to Mark 11:24, I'm healed!" The nurses all just shook their heads sympathetically, because they knew the doctors had said she'd be dead in ten days. The aunt even told one of the doctors, "According to Mark 11:24, I'm healed!"

Several days went by, and the aunt couldn't tell any outward difference in her condition. But every day, she was getting better. And

after ten days, instead of dying, doctors said, "We don't understand it. The cancer has just disappeared!"

This woman just had faith in what God said in His Word:
When you pray, believe you receive!

You know, we've never fathomed the depth of faith—the depth
of what believing God can produce in a person's life. There's
just something about believing God. Smith Wigglesworth said,
"There's something about believing God that'll cause God to pass
over a million people just to get to you."

THE ANOINTING AND FAITH IN THE WORD EACH YIELD THE SAME RESULTS—HEALING!

I'm still explaining the difference between receiving healing
through the healing anointing and receiving the same results
without the healing anointing, but just by simple faith in God's
Word.

Now it is true that a person who's specially anointed can minister healing with the anointing of God. When he does, he is conscious of the Presence of God—the Spirit of God. In other words,
the power of God is *upon* him and *in* him, and that power can be
transmitted from one person to another.

For instance, we looked at the personal testimony of the woman
with the issue of blood. That testimony goes into detail or talks
specifically about a transfer of power or healing anointing.

MARK 5:25-30

25 And a certain woman, which had an issue of blood twelve years,

26 And had suffered many things of many physicians, and had spent all that she had [all of her living], and was nothing bettered, but rather grew worse,

27 When she had heard of Jesus, came in the press behind, and touched his garment [His clothes].

28 For she said, If I may touch but his clothes, I shall be whole.

29 And straightway the fountain of her blood was dried up; and she felt in her body that she was healed of that plague.

30 And Jesus, immediately knowing in himself that VIRTUE [the Greek says "power"] HAD GONE OUT OF HIM, turned him about in the press, and said, Who touched my clothes?

So this case talks about a transfer of power—Holy Ghost healing power or *anointing*!

Well, really, all biblical or scriptural healings come under one of two main headings (but there may be many *sub*headings!): 1) healed by the power of God—by the transference of healing power or anointing; and 2) healed by faith in the Word of God.

Now let me give you some more illustrations that show the difference between receiving healing by the healing anointing or *Holy Ghost power* and receiving healing through simple faith in God's Word with no special anointing in manifestation.

HEALED THROUGH THE HEALING ANOINTING

You remember I said Jesus appeared to me in that first vision in 1950 in Rockwall, Texas. He laid the finger of His right hand in the palm of each one of my hands, and He laid His hand on my head and said, "I have called thee and have anointed thee and have given unto thee a special anointing to minister to the sick."

Well, afterward, I was conscious of that anointing. When it was in manifestation, it felt like I was holding a coal of fire in both hands.

So in Oklahoma, in the very next meeting I held after the Rockwall vision, a minister from Arkansas brought his wife to one of the services for prayer. They'd been in an automobile accident seven years before, and she'd experienced a severe head injury and had been blind ever since the accident.

She told me, "I can't tell if it's daylight or dark. If someone was standing in front of me in the light, I could tell that something was there, but it would be just sort of a semi-dark figure to me."

In other words, she would be able to see an image if something were there in front of her, but she wouldn't be able to tell if it was a man, woman, horse, cow, or automobile. That's pretty blind, isn't it!

Well, I laid my hands on her two blind eyes in that service, and I was conscious of the healing power going into her eyes.

So I related that to her and said, "Now Sister, Jesus said that if you'll believe that I'm anointed, and if you'll receive that anointing, the anointing will effect a healing and a cure. So you are to *expect*." I was talking to her while I had my hands on her eyes.

In the church where we were, there was a placard on the wall with writing on it that said "Prayer Changes Things."

I said to this woman, "Faith is an act. If you received the healing anointing and could see—and the healing anointing *has* gone into you—you would be able to read, wouldn't you?"

"Sure," she said.

"All right," I said, "the first thing you do when I take my hands off your eyes is start looking, because there's a sign on the wall in front of you. I want you to read it."

I took my hands off her eyes, and it was quite obvious that for a second or two, she couldn't see a thing. But, suddenly, her face lit up like a neon sign in the dark and she said, "I see it! I see it! I see it! It says 'Prayer changes things'!"

I reached back to the pulpit and picked up a songbook. I opened it and handed it to her and said, "Read those verses." She read them.

I took my Bible, just opened it at random, and handed it to her and said, "Read these scriptures." She just began reading them off!

This woman was instantly healed with that healing anointing. She was healed through her faith in the healing power of God.

HEALING THROUGH SIMPLE FAITH IN THE WORD

Now in that same meeting, another minister and his wife told me, "We're going to bring a lady from our church to one of your services who has not walked a step in four years. Doctors said she'll never walk again." So they brought her to the meeting.

Well, in that particular service, before I ever reached this crippled woman in the healing line, the healing anointing had dissipated. I don't know whether or not you understand that. I alluded to it earlier, but there is an anointing to heal just like there is an anointing to preach.

LUKE 4:18

18 The Spirit of the Lord is upon me, because he hath anointed me
    to PREACH [or teach] the gospel to the poor; he hath sent me to
    HEAL ....

For example, a minister will make preparation through prayer and study to preach. When he gets before the people and starts out ministering in faith, the anointing to preach will come upon him, and he preaches until that anointing lifts (however, some preachers keep going after the anointing lifts!).

The anointing to preach is potentially *present* all the time, but it is not *in manifestation* all the time. If the anointing to preach were in manifestation all the time, a minister would just never stop preaching. He would preach himself to death—he'd just keep on preaching till he died.

In the same way, the healing anointing is potentially present all the time, but it's not *in manifestation* all the time. And when a minister who's anointed with the healing power grows tired, it's more difficult for him to yield to the Spirit. The minister is a vessel or channel, so to speak, through which the Holy Ghost flows. As we already found out, the Holy Ghost power flows a lot like electricity. And electricity is a power in the natural that also needs a channel or conduit through which to flow.

In Mark chapter 5, in the case of the woman with the issue of blood, there was an outflow of power from Jesus to the woman, and Jesus was aware of that outflow, because He said, "Power has gone out of Me. Who touched Me?" (v. 30). And the woman, too, was aware of the reception of power (vv. 29, 33).

And so, concerning the healing anointing or power, I'm just honest with people who come to the healing line to have hands laid on them. If the healing anointing is no longer in manifestation, I tell them, "The anointing's gone. I'm not going to lie to you. I can't minister to you the way I ministered to the others before the anointing dissipated. But I *can* lay my hands on you in faith just like any layman could do, because the Bible said believers shall lay hands on the sick and they shall recover" (Mark 16:18).

There were a lot of people in the healing line during that service the crippled woman attended. I laid my hands on many of them with the healing anointing and was conscious of the anointing flowing into those individuals.

But about one-fourth of the people in the line hadn't been prayed for when I said to them, "The anointing's gone. If you want me to minister to you with the *anointing*, you'll have to come back tomorrow night, because I just don't have it anymore tonight. And I'm not going to lie to you and tell you that I do. But if you can't come back tomorrow night, just stay in the line, and I'll lay hands on you in faith."

The minister and his wife who'd brought the crippled woman to be prayed for had driven a great distance to be in the service, and they couldn't come back the next night. So this minister and some others carried the crippled lady over to where I was standing.

I had to deal with this woman on the basis of faith alone by just opening the Bible, having her read some scriptures on healing, and then having her act upon God's Word for herself.

Well, I did, she did, and God did! Praise God! Right there in front of everybody, that woman who hadn't walked a step in four years leaped to her feet and danced and jumped and was healed!

Now the blind woman was healed in the same meeting through a transfer of power or anointing. But the crippled woman was healed just by faith in God's Word. She received healing by acting upon God's Word. Yet they both got the same results—*healing.*

Faith will cause God to move on your behalf. Yet on the other hand, it's true that we need to learn to minister with the anointing—the healing anointing—and learn something about its operation. But whether or not the tangible healing power of God is in manifestation, you can have faith for healing and *receive* your healing through faith in the anointed Word!

—Chapter 6—

MINISTERING WITH THE HEALING ANOINTING

Then he answered and spake unto me, saying, This is the word of the Lord unto Zerubbabel, saying, Not by might, nor by power, but by my spirit, saith the Lord of hosts.

—Zechariah 4:6

. . . and the YOKE shall be destroyed because of the anointing.

—Isaiah 10:27

We've already said that sickness is a yoke (if you don't know that sickness is a yoke, you've never been sick!). And we said that just as a person could be a *spiritual* captive, he could be a *physical* captive too. But Luke 4:18 said, *"The Spirit of the Lord is upon me, because he hath anointed me . . . to preach DELIVERANCE to the CAPTIVES . . . ."* There is deliverance and healing through the yoke-destroying anointing!

Through the years, many preachers have ministered healing in various ways under the anointing of the Spirit of God. Yet I'm of the opinion that, really, none of us knows as much as we should about the healing anointing. But the more we begin to see what the Word of God says about the anointing, and the more we yield to the Holy Spirit and learn from Him, the more we'll know and the more effective we will be.

We need to explore all the avenues of biblical healing, not just one or two. We know God heals. And we understand, of course, that we can just pray according to the Word and believe that we receive healing right then *when we pray* and yet not have any kind of immediate manifestation. Many people are healed that way. That's the way I was healed—by simply believing I received my healing according to the Word.

But then there is also such a thing as receiving healing by having the healing anointing ministered to you. As I said, we need to study the healing anointing, especially in the ministry of Jesus.

You see, even when we minister with the healing anointing (and God wants some of us to do that), we may not all minister the same way. And sometimes when something is done a little differently from the way people have seen it done, even though we have scripture for it, it gets criticized because people don't understand it.

When the Lord first appeared to me in 1950 in a tent meeting in Rockwall, Texas, as everybody in the meeting was praying around the altar, I heard a Voice in the English language say, "Come up hither." I heard it three times, and then the fourth time the Voice said, "Come up hither; come up to the Throne of God." I opened my eyes and saw Jesus standing about where the top of the tent should have been.

It seemed like I just went right up there and stood with Him. He said, "Let's go up to the throne of God." And we went up and stood before God's throne.

In the process of time, Jesus laid the finger of His right hand in the palm of each one of my hands. When He did, my palms began to burn just like I was holding a coal of fire in them. I don't mean I felt just a warmth; I felt *heat* in the palms of my hands.

Then Jesus said, "Kneel before Me." I knelt before Him, and He laid His hand on my head and said, "I've called thee and have anointed thee, and have given unto thee a special anointing to minister to the sick."

The entire vision lasted about an hour-and-a-half. All the people who were present praying around the altar heard my part of the conversation that I'd had with Jesus. So no one left because they were extremely interested in finding out about it!

Now the pastor who had rented the tent and asked me to be the guest speaker was also an official with his particular Full Gospel denomination. The vision took place in September on a Saturday night. We closed the meeting on Sunday night. Then on Tuesday of the following week, this pastor went to a meeting with other officials of his denomination to plan a special Bible conference for the fall.

This pastor was so thrilled about what happened at our meeting that he shared with the other ministers concerning the vision I'd had.

This pastor said to me later, "Brother Hagin, to my astonishment, nearly all of them were against it! They were almost ready to call you on the carpet, take your fellowship papers away from you, and turn you out of the denomination for having a vision!"

They were going to turn me out for seeing Jesus and for feeling the power of God in my hands!

Finally the chairman of the meeting spoke up in my defense. He said, "Men, wait a minute. Now first of all, let me ask you all a question. Does anyone here know how the power felt that went out of Jesus and into the woman with the issue of blood that we read about in the Bible?"

He continued: "Jesus was anointed. And that anointing did flow out of Him and into that woman, and it healed her." Then he asked them again, "Do any of you know how that anointing felt?"

Well, none of them knew. Then the chairman said, "Besides that, I know Brother Hagin personally. He pastored in my area, not just for a few months, but for years.

"And let me say this: Through my contact with Brother Hagin all these years, my experience with him has been nothing but good. He was the most spiritual one among us. He lived the most holy life of any minister we had. He was the most disciplined.

"In fact, Brother Hagin lives such a good and upright life that I personally would believe anything he said. If he said the sun was going to rise in the west in the morning, I'd get out of bed in the morning looking west!"

Those were the chairman's words, not mine, but I certainly appreciated him standing up for me like that.

The minister who was relating all this to me said, "When the chairman said that, the rest of them said, 'Well, we guess we'd better forget about it then.'"

You know, it is good to live right, isn't it! Folks will have more confidence in you when you live holy before God.

DON'T BACK OFF FROM MINISTERING WITH THE ANOINTING

Well, as time went on, I began to minister with that same anointing Jesus anointed me with when I had the vision in Rockwall. I was holding a meeting for one pastor, and another pastor in the same town got upset with me. He was mad because he didn't like the fact that I was anointed! He didn't like the fact that the healing power of God was flowing out of me and into others!

So this pastor called a special meeting of the committee that oversaw the denomination's operations in that area of the state. At the meeting, he said, "I think we ought to just call Brother Hagin in and turn him out of the denomination for claiming to feel the power of God in his hands and for claiming that he saw Jesus."

Well, I'd preached revival meetings at the churches of every member of that committee. And every one of them spoke up and said, "We're all one hundred percent in favor of calling Brother Hagin in to see if he'll hold us *another* revival!"

I felt no animosity toward the pastor who had called that meeting. He came to me and shook hands with me at another meeting and said, "I'll say one thing about you, Brother Hagin. You left a good taste in the mouth of every pastor you preached for."

You know, you don't have to go around advertising a lot of things about your ministry. If you'll just live right, and if those things about your ministry are really so, the Lord will back you up.

WHAT FOLKS ARE NOT 'UP' ON, THEY'RE 'DOWN' ON!

I was preaching in another state a couple of years later. I was only in my early thirties, and the pastor there was almost ready to retire. He said to me, "Brother Hagin, a number of years ago, God tried to use me the same way He's using you. I had almost identically the same kind of experience you had. And I began to minister that way. But some of the brethren talked me out of it, and I laid it all down. Don't you let anybody talk you out of what you've received from the Lord. You stay with it."

Well, I was determined to stay with it anyway, but that minister just wanted to encourage me.

The very next year, another minister in another state said almost the same thing to me. I was preaching in his particular state, and there was quite a bit of controversy over doctrine among the church people in that area. It was like someone once described: "What folks are not *up* on, they're *down* on."

The pastor of the church where I was ministering was about seventy-some-odd years of age. He said to me, "Brother Hagin, I was in the healing ministry too. I started back there with John Alexander Dowie before the turn of the century. I was also there at the beginning of the Pentecostal Movement when there was such an outpouring of the Holy Ghost.

"God tried to use me the same way He uses you," this pastor continued, "but I let some of the brethren talk me out of it. Don't you let anybody talk you out of it, no matter who they are."

Well, I had great confidence in a man of his caliber, but I was already determined not to let anyone talk me out of what the Lord had told me to do.

Thank God for the privilege of simply obeying the Lord! But when you do obey the Lord, the devil will throw up every road-block he can. Yet it pays to just stay faithful to God.

I never criticized those fellows who tried to talk me out of the anointing. They didn't know any better. Actually, I didn't know very much about the anointing myself.

Why don't we know more about this subject? The only reason we don't know more about a particular Bible subject is, we've never studied along that particular line. Yet all the while, the healing anointing has been in the scriptures.

Naturally, after the Lord appeared to me in 1950, I began to study some about the healing anointing because I want to prove everything by the scriptures. I became satisfied in my own heart, so I continued to preach along that line from time to time.

Then later, the Lord spoke to me and said, "Study further about the anointing." So I began to study even further, and the more I studied about it, I began to understand more clearly certain things that I'd already seen to some extent in the past.

We already know that one can be anointed with this healing power. But a person can't anoint himself, and people can't anoint each other. We read, *"How GOD anointed Jesus of Nazareth . . ."* (Acts 10:38). And we read, *"GOD wrought special miracles by the hands of Paul"* (Acts 19:11). So we know that it's *God* who does the work. And, of course, He does it through Jesus, who is the Head of the Church.

THE SPIRIT WITHIN AND UPON

The anointing comes *upon* people to enable them to do whatever God asks them to do. Jesus said that in the Gospels: *"The Spirit of the Lord is UPON me, because he hath anointed me"* (Luke 4:18).

Now there is an anointing of the Spirit that is *within* every believer, but it's not for him to minister with. It's for his own personal benefit. For instance, First John 2:27 said, *"But the anointing which ye have received of him abideth IN you . . . the same anointing teacheth you of all things, and is truth, and is no lie, and even as it hath taught you, ye shall abide in him."*

So the anointing *within* is a different anointing than the anointing that comes *upon* someone. It's the same Spirit, but it is a different *anointing*. The anointing that can come *upon* you even feels different.

And you remember we said a person cannot anoint himself. A lot of Christians have tried to anoint themselves for ministry, but they can't do it. God has to be the One who does it (Acts 10:38).

Concerning the anointing in the ministry of Jesus, we can see that for a while, Jesus was the only representative of God, anointed of God, ministering upon the earth. Later Jesus called unto Himself the Twelve, the disciples, and said, "I give you power" (Matt. 10:1; Mark 6:7).

MARK 6:7, 12-13

7 And he called unto him the twelve, and began to send them forth by two and two; and GAVE THEM POWER over unclean spirits.

12 And they went out, and PREACHED that men should repent.

13 And they cast out many devils, and anointed with oil many that were sick, and HEALED them.

Verse 7 says Jesus gave the disciples power. Well, you can't give somebody something you don't have. But Jesus had power to cast out devils and to heal the sick, and so He gave the disciples that power.

Then later on, Jesus called another seventy disciples, gave them power, and sent them out too (Luke 10:1). He sent them out with that same Holy Ghost power.

Remember we said a person is anointed by God to accomplish a work that God has for him to do. In other words, the anointing comes *upon* a person to stand in a particular office or to fulfill a particular calling.

Now the twelve disciples, the seventy, and we as Christians are all in the *same* Body, the Body of Jesus Christ who is the Head of the Church. But when it comes to ministry, we're not all in the same *office* (Rom. 12:4).

Whatever office God has called you to, He will anoint you to stand in that office and to perform that ministry. Now there are some things you can do to cause that anointing to become stronger and in greater manifestation, such as doing a little fasting and a little extra praying—a little extra waiting on God. But if you're anointed by God to stand in a particular office, you will always have a *measure* of that anointing.

THE ANOINTING TO HEAL VS. THE ANOINTING TO PREACH OR TEACH

In studying about the anointing, we've discovered that the healing power of God is a tangible substance. It is a *heavenly materiality*. That's about the best way to describe it, because the word "tangible" means *perceptible to the touch* or *capable of being touched.* So we know this healing anointing *must* be tangible because it can be touched or felt.

Those who are in the ministry know something about the anointing that comes upon them to teach or to preach. That anointing to preach or teach is tangible because, after all, the same Spirit who anoints people to minister healing also anoints people to preach and teach. You remember in Luke 4, Jesus was anointed to *speak*—to preach and teach—and to *heal.*

But the anointing to speak is a different *type* of anointing than the healing anointing. And yet, a minister can feel the anointing to preach or teach because it's tangible, and it's the same Spirit who anoints him.

In my own experience, I've gone to the pulpit at times when the anointing to minister was on me so strong, it seemed like I was just jumping and jerking inside. In other words, the anointing just *vibrated* within me; I could *feel* it.

When the anointing is on you to preach or teach, that anointing goes out of you, and your words go out of your mouth freighted with the Holy Ghost, impregnated with the power of God. And others feel it. Why? Because those words are laden with the Spirit.

But now we're talking about the healing anointing. The healing anointing is very similar to the anointing to preach and teach. The healing anointing, too, is perceptible to the touch or capable of being touched.

THERE IS AN ANOINTING ESPECIALLY TO MINISTER TO THE SICK

We've talked about the difference between the anointing that's *within* every believer and the anointing for ministry that comes *upon* certain believers who are called of God. Yet there is still another difference between the anointing that comes upon a person to perform a certain ministry and a *special* anointing, such as the healing anointing, that can also come upon a minister.

The anointing for ministry automatically comes with the calling to stand in whatever office God has called you to. But the *healing anointing* is something different and separate from a *ministry anointing.*

For instance, Jesus said to me when He appeared to me in the vision in Rockwall, Texas, in 1950: "I have called you before you were born. I separated you unto the ministry from your mother's womb. Satan tried to destroy your life before you were born and many times since then, but My angels have watched over you and have cared for you until this present hour."

Well, when Jesus said, "I have called you," that didn't mean He called me on that very day, September 2, 1950. He had called me to the ministry before I was born. I understood what He meant when He said, "I have called you."

After Jesus said, "I have called you," He said, "and I have anointed you." Well, again, I knew He wasn't talking about anointing me for the ministry that very day. No, the anointing came with the calling, and I'd already been ministering with that anointing for many years.

But then when Jesus said to me, "And I have given unto you a *special* anointing to lay hands on the sick," I knew He was talking about giving me a *special* anointing on that very day, September 2, 1950.

Now I had been laying hands on the sick for years and had seen them healed. But I wasn't ministering with a special anointing; I was just ministering to the sick through the laying on of hands according to the Word.

After Jesus gave me a special anointing in that vision to lay hands on the sick, He said to me, "Stand upright on your feet" (Jesus had told me to kneel, and I had been kneeling throughout the vision).

Then Jesus said to me, among other things, "This special anointing will not work unless you tell the people exactly what I've told you. Tell the people that you saw Me. Tell them exactly what I told you, and tell them if they'll *believe* it—that you're anointed— and *receive* it, then that power will flow. The anointing will work for them."

You see, the healing power *flows*. And it also works by faith. For example, in the case of the woman with the issue of blood, that power flowed out of Jesus into her. Jesus said, "Daughter, thy faith hath made thee whole."

Notice she was the only one out of the whole crowd who got healed. The Bible says a crowd or multitude was thronging Jesus (Mark 5:31). And Jesus was anointed with that healing power the entire time, yet she was the only one out of the crowd who the Bible said received healing.

Have you ever been in the midst of a multitude? The Bible said the woman with the issue of blood "came in the press behind" (Mark 5:27). Well, "press" means they were pressing in on every side against Jesus! And in the midst of all that, Jesus said, "Somebody touched Me."

The power that Jesus was anointed with didn't just flow out from Jesus to everybody. Yet it flowed out to this woman when she touched His clothes. What caused that power to flow out of Him into her? *Her faith.*

That's the way the anointing works. There may be a multitude of people and yet just one of them receive healing. Of course, all of them *could* receive if the anointing is present or in manifestation. They could believe God and be healed by the transfer of power. (Or even if the anointing isn't present, they could believe God and receive healing according to His Word, just by faith.)

You see, certain things cause the anointing to work, and certain things, such as unbelief, will keep it from working. The anointing doesn't just work automatically.

YOU HAVE TO RESPOND TO THE ANOINTING FOR IT TO BENEFIT YOU

Many times people have thought, "Well, if the Holy Ghost is going to do something, He'll just do it." But that's not true. People have to *respond* to the Holy Ghost.

For example, Jesus said in John 6:44, *"No man can come to me, except the Father which hath sent me draw him."* Well, the way the Father does that is through the Holy Ghost.

The Holy Ghost may be present in a church service, for example, drawing sinners to the Father. But the Holy Ghost doesn't grab them by the hair and jerk them to the altar! No, sinners have to *respond* to the Holy Ghost.

You see, man has his part to play in responding to the Spirit of God or the anointing. The healing anointing can be present to help someone, but if that person doesn't respond, the anointing will just be there, *ineffective*, as far as that person is concerned.

SCRIPTURAL PRECEDENCE FOR THE SPECIAL ANOINTING TODAY

When Jesus said to me in the Rockwall vision, "I have called you and have anointed you and have given unto you a special anointing to minister to the sick," He also gave me the scriptures Acts 19:11 and 12:

ACTS 19:11-12

11 And God wrought special miracles by the hands of Paul:

12 So that from his body were brought unto the sick handkerchiefs or aprons, and the diseases departed from them, and the evil spirits went out of them.

Well, the way God wrought special miracles by the hands of Paul was by specially anointing him.

Then Jesus said something else to me in this vision. He said, "If I want to do anything special by *your* hands [talking about giving me that special anointing], I don't have to get the church members together and have them to vote on it to see whether I can or not."

JESUS IS THE HEAD OF THE CHURCH

Jesus is the Head of the Church or the Body of Christ. We are the Body, and He is the Head. In Romans chapter 12, the Apostle

Paul uses the human body as an illustration of the Body of Christ. Well, in the natural, your head controls the rest of your body. Your head doesn't say, "I'm going to get all my fingers and toes together and have them vote." No, the head controls the body.

What I'm saying to you is this: Jesus is still distributing offices and ministries and anointings. You remember, He called the Twelve to Himself and authorized them and sent them out. Later He called the seventy and authorized them. It says He gave them power (Luke 10:1, 19).

So Jesus is the Head. He is the One who distributes ministries and anointings. And God planned it that way. In other words, the Bible doesn't say *God* is the Head of the Church. It says *Jesus* is (Eph. 1:22). No, Jesus is not usurping any authority over the Father; that's just the way God planned it—for *Jesus* to be Head of the Church.

Now in chapters 14, 15, and 16 of John's Gospel, we read what Jesus the Head of the Church said about the Holy Ghost. One thing Jesus said that's especially interesting is that the Holy Ghost will not speak of Himself. He speaks of Jesus.

JOHN 16:13-14

13 Howbeit when he, the Spirit of truth, is come, he will guide you into all truth: for HE SHALL NOT SPEAK OF HIMSELF; but whatsoever he shall hear, that shall he speak: and he will shew you things to come.

14 He shall glorify me: for he shall receive of mine, and shall shew it unto you.

The Holy Ghost never speaks of Himself. But He takes the things of Jesus and shows them to us. And whatsoever He hears from Jesus, that shall He speak.

And so you see, Jesus is still distributing ministries. He's the Head of the Church, setting offices in the Body, anointing people, and disbursing the anointing.

HEBREWS 2:4

4 God also bearing them [the early apostles] witness, both with signs and wonders, and with divers miracles, and GIFTS of the Holy Ghost, according to his own will.

You could miss what the writer of Hebrews is saying here if you automatically think that when you read the word "gift" or "gifts" in the New Testament, it always means the same thing. There are four different Greek words translated "gifts" in the New Testament.

In the margin of my Bible, it says that this phrase "gifts of the Holy Ghost" could also be read "*distributions* of the Holy Ghost." And the Greek word translated "gifts" in Hebrews 2:4 means *miraculous faculty* or *endowment*.

So God distributes the miraculous faculty or endowment of the Holy Ghost (for ministry, not for the New Birth) "according to His own will" (Heb. 2:4). According to *whose* will? *My* will? *Your* will? The *Holy Ghost's* will? No. God distributes those miraculous endowments according to *His* will and *Jesus'* will, because Jesus is the Head of the Church!

That's the reason Jesus said to me, "I don't have to get the church members together and have them to vote on it to see whether or not I can give you this special anointing. I'm the Head of the Church."

In other words, Jesus didn't have to ask any man for permission to distribute any anointings. He didn't have to get the church to form a committee and have them work it all out. Why didn't He? Because He is the Head of the Church!

So Jesus told me in effect, "If I want to do anything through your hands, I don't have to call a special meeting to vote on it."

Jesus gave me that special anointing because He is the Head of the Church. And He is still distributing special anointings today, according to His own will.

THE HOLY GHOST POWER FLOWS

Now how does this special anointing operate? How is a person who's anointed going to get that healing power over to someone else? Well, one thing about it, we know that this power *flows*.

As I mentioned before, electricity is God's power in the natural realm, but Holy Ghost power is God's power in the spirit realm.

After men discovered electricity, at first they didn't know how to get it to flow. They didn't know the rules and laws that governed it. But they finally learned about them and found out how they could get electricity to flow!

For instance, not just any metal will conduct electricity. And similarly, you'll find that not just any kind of substance or material will conduct the *Holy Ghost* power.

In the case of the woman with the issue of blood, it was cloth— Jesus' clothes—that conducted that power. We could say that the Holy Ghost power flowed like electricity out of Jesus into the woman. Or we could use another analogy and say that the Holy Ghost power flows like *water* flows.

That's thoroughly scriptural, because Jesus Himself said it in John's Gospel.

JOHN 7:37–39

37 In the last day, that great day of the feast, Jesus stood and cried, saying, If any man thirst, let him come unto me, and drink.

38 He that believeth on me, as the scripture hath said, out of his belly shall FLOW RIVERS of LIVING WATER.

39 (But this spake he of THE SPIRIT, which they that believe on him should receive: for the Holy Ghost was not yet given; because that Jesus was not yet glorified.)

In verse 37, Jesus said, *"If any man thirst, let him come unto me, and drink."* Well, when you think about thirst and drinking, you think about *water*! Then verse 38 says that out of his belly or innermost being shall flow *rivers.* That's talking about water. Have you ever seen *sand* flowing in a river? No, not unless the sand is in water, because *water* flows in rivers!

What is this water? Verse 39 tells us: *"But this spake he of the SPIRIT, which they that believe on him should receive: for the HOLY GHOST was not yet given; because that Jesus was not yet glorified.*" So then we can readily say that Holy Ghost power, the anointing, flows like water.

Of course, in the time of Jesus' earthly ministry, Jesus couldn't use the illustration of electricity to describe the operation of the anointing because people wouldn't have known what He was talking about! But they knew about water!

THE TRANSFER OF HOLY GHOST POWER

The Holy Spirit flows like electricity, and the Holy Spirit flows like water. We know a person can't anoint himself with this Holy Spirit power. God does the anointing, but the transmittable, transferable anointing can flow from one person to another.

We read about the transmittable anointing in the case of Elijah and Elisha in Second Kings 2:9 and 15. And evidently, a similar thing happened when Jesus called unto Himself the twelve disciples and gave them authority or power (Matt. 10:1).

Since Jesus had the Spirit or the anointing without measure, He called unto Himself the Twelve and sent them forth. He said, "I give *you* power." Well, where did Jesus get the power? *"GOD ANOINTED Jesus of Nazareth with the Holy Ghost and with power*(Acts 10:38).

God anointed Jesus. That's where Jesus got the power— from God!

We said that it is *God* who does the anointing. A person can't anoint himself for ministry or just decide to anoint someone else. But very often in ministry, the anointing *is transferred* from one person to another, as in the case of Elijah and Elisha or Jesus and the Twelve and the seventy. The Word of God said something else about this in the Old Testament, referring to Moses and Joshua.

DEUTERONOMY 31:14, 23

14 And the Lord said unto Moses, Behold, thy days approach that thou must die: call Joshua, and present yourselves in the tabernacle of the congregation, that I may give him a charge. And Moses and Joshua went, and presented themselves in the tabernacle of the congregation . . . .

23 And he [Moses] gave Joshua the son of Nun a charge, and said, Be strong and of a good courage: for thou shalt bring the children of Israel into the land which I sware unto them: and I will be with thee.

DEUTERONOMY 34:9

9 And Joshua the son of Nun was FULL OF THE SPIRIT OF WISDOM; for Moses had LAID HIS HANDS UPON HIM: and the children of Israel hearkened unto him, and did as the Lord commanded Moses.

Joshua had the same spirit of wisdom that Moses had, for Moses had laid his hands upon Joshua. Well, evidently some of the same spiritual wisdom and power of God that Moses was anointed with was transferred to Joshua by the laying on of hands.

The power of God is transferable. We've seen that in the Gospels: *"And when he* [Jesus] *had called unto him his twelve disciples, he gave them POWER against unclean spirits, to cast them out, and to heal all manner of sickness and all manner of disease"* (Matt. 10:1).

I know the Greek word for power here is also translated *authority*, but right on the other hand, whether it's *authority* or literal *power*, how did the disciples heal the sick and cast out devils? *By the power of God!*

JESUS MINISTERED PRIMARILY BY THE HEALING POWER

That's primarily how Jesus healed the sick and cast out devils—by the anointing or the healing power of God. And since Jesus healed the sick and cast out devils through the anointing, how was He going to send His disciples out to do the same things? Was He going to send them out to heal the sick and cast out devils with their own power?

Were the disciples going out with human power to do the same works Jesus did just because Jesus said, "Do it"? No, if they could have done that, they would have already been doing it. They had to receive *Holy Ghost power* to do the works of Jesus.

THE BALANCE OF FAITH AND POWER

Now here's something very interesting that's going to bring us back to a thought which I established previously. (That's one reason I keep going over some of the same things, approaching them from a different angle. This is new ground to most of us, and I want you to see it.)

Jesus authorized and evidently empowered the apostles to go out and do the works we just talked about. But notice something else here. The apostles ran across another fellow whom Jesus *didn't* empower, yet this other fellow was doing the same works.

One of the disciples said to Jesus, *"Master, we saw one casting out devils IN THY NAME, and he followeth not us: and we forbad him, because he followeth not us"* (Mark 9:38).

Jesus said, *"Forbid him not: for there is no man which shall do a miracle in my name, that can lightly speak evil of me"* (Mark 9:39).

Jesus didn't empower this fellow, but Jesus said, "Forbid him not." You see, this fellow wasn't empowered *per se*; he was just casting out devils *by faith*. He'd probably been in some of Jesus' services and saw Jesus doing it. So the man just had faith, bless God, to get after it and cast out devils! And he did it by faith.

This fellow the disciples saw casting out devils was a stranger to the disciples. Jesus hadn't called him like He'd called the others. Jesus hadn't said, "I authorize you; I give you power." No, this fellow was casting out devils by faith in the Name of Jesus. He was just doing it by faith!

EXAMPLES OF DELIVERANCE THROUGH THE WORD OF FAITH

I remember something along this line that John G. Lake said years ago. Almost all the denominations had missionaries in South Africa, and John Lake was invited to go to Africa to visit a group of these missionaries.

These missionaries were greatly disturbed because they'd been unsuccessful in dealing with the witch doctors' witchcraft power. Many of the missionaries were ready to give up in despair. They said, "What are we going to do? These witch doctors exercise great power." And the witch doctors did do phenomenal, miraculous things.

So John Lake said to the missionaries. "Well, why don't you cast the devil out of them?" (Lake was just that kind of person; he was very forthright.)

One Christian missionary replied half-jokingly, "Cast the devil out of *them*? Why, they'll cast the devil out of *you*!" In other words, this missionary wasn't saying that Lake had a devil in him; he was saying the witch doctors had more power than Lake.

Lake said, "They don't have more power than I do, because greater is He that's in me than he that's in the world!" (1 John 4:4).

By invitation, Lake would go to worldwide spiritist or spiritualist meetings, where thousands of people would be in attendance. Lake would say, "I'll come if you'll give me two hours to address the people." Then he'd go to those occult meetings and talk about the power of God for two hours!

Lake would say, "You people are acquainted with phenomenal spirit activities in the spirit realm. Let's see you do a bigger miracle than I can do." He was bold about it, bless God, because he knew the Greater One—the Holy Ghost—was in him! The Greater One is greater than all the devils and demons put together.

Lake once told about being in Africa in the bush country where a chieftain said to him, "I heard a witch doctor say he was going to put a curse on another chieftain on Sunday and that the chieftain would die."

So Lake rode on horseback as fast as he could to reach that chieftain by Sunday, the day the witch doctor had said he was going to put the curse on him. It took Lake two days to reach the chieftain.

It was a custom with these chieftains to go out and look their flocks over. It was Sunday entertainment with them to go out and count their cows.

Lake said, "I rode out to see the flock with this chieftain who was going to be cursed by the witch doctor. And suddenly, he began to get hot all over." (The witch doctor, miles away, had said: "On Sunday I'm gonna burn him up.")

Well, the chieftain began to get warm, then hot, and he began taking his clothes off to try to cool down. Then, suddenly, the chieftain sort of passed out and fell off of his horse.

Lake, who knew something about science and medicine, said, "From all observation, it looked like the chieftain was about to have a stroke. His face was red all over."

Lake continued, "I just wanted to see if that witch doctor over there from many miles away could actually put a curse on someone. Then I saw that the attack had gone far enough. There was no doubt in my mind that the chieftain would die. So I grabbed hold of him and said, 'In the Name of Jesus Christ, I break this thing!'"

In the Name of Jesus Christ, Lake commanded the devil and all his cohorts to leave, and the man rose up well and all right!

Now Lake was a man who was anointed, but he didn't break that demonic power with the anointing; he did it by faith, in the Name of Jesus. He spoke the Word.

Yes, the Name of Jesus is greater than every name or any name that is named in three worlds—Heaven, earth, and hell! Hallelujah! God raised Jesus from the dead and gave Him a Name that is above every name (Phil. 2:9)!

Philippians 2:10 says, *"That at the name of Jesus every knee should bow, of things IN HEAVEN, and things IN EARTH, and things UNDER THE EARTH."* That means angels, men, and devils. Just believe that, because it's Bible!

Smith Wigglesworth was also a man anointed of God, and he, too, ministered under the anointing, but not always.

Wigglesworth lived in England. He tells about the time a mother and daddy contacted him. Their young married daughter had lost her mind. They phoned Wigglesworth, sent him a telegram, and wrote him a letter to see if he would come help them.

Wigglesworth didn't just go anywhere and everywhere he was asked to go. If he did, he'd have been on the go all the time. But when God told him to go, he went.

Well, the Lord told Wigglesworth to go visit that mother and daddy, so he simply wrote them a note saying he'd be there on such-and-such day at ten o'clock in the morning.

When Wigglesworth arrived, he rang the doorbell of their palatial home, and the couple opened the door. They never said a word. One of them took Wigglesworth by one hand, the other one took him by the other hand, and they led him down a hallway and up a flight of stairs to a closed door.

The daddy of the young girl who'd lost her mind pushed open the door. Then both he and the mother stepped back, leaving Wigglesworth standing in the doorway. Wigglesworth looked inside the room and saw a beautiful young lady with five grown men holding her down. The woman looked toward Wigglesworth, wild-eyed, and just thrust the five grown men away from her!

Five grown men could not hold this girl down! Many times when demon power is in operation, the people through whom the demon power is operating have supernatural or super-human strength.

After this young girl rose up and tore herself loose from the five grown men, she faced Wigglesworth, her eyes blazing. "You can't cast me out!" a voice said, because that devil had taken her over and was using her voice.

Wigglesworth said, "Jesus can. And in the Name of Jesus Christ of Nazareth, come out of her!"

Thirty-seven devils came out, giving a name. Afterwards, the young girl's mind was perfectly restored. She walked down the stairs and had the evening meal with her family.

Somebody said to Wigglesworth, "What's your secret?" (If you could learn his secret, you could do the same thing!)

"How did you do it?" the person asked.

"Oh," he said, "I just remembered that the Bible said greater is He that's in me than he that's in the world" (1 John 4:4).

You see, that's a matter of faith, not a matter of anointing. Now don't misunderstand me, at times Wigglesworth did operate under the anointing. But in that particular instance, he just remembered, "Greater is He that's in me; I don't care how many devils are in her, He that's in me is greater!"

So, you see, we need to learn about faith. You and I can't always operate under the anointing. But we *can* always operate in faith, anointing or no anointing, because we've got God's Word.

Faith in God's Word always works—every day, every time, every hour. Faith in God's Word is best. That's the reason I put the Word first. I always teach faith in God's Word first, but we don't want to leave out the other, the anointing. God wants us to understand the operation of the healing anointing.

You see, when you're just operating in faith, you can cast out spirits. But did you notice in the scriptures we've studied that under the ministry of Jesus, those with unclean spirits were healed or made whole. That means they were delivered.

In those particular instances, it *didn't* say, "Jesus cast the spirits out with His Word" as it does in other places. No, it said, *"And the whole multitude sought to touch him: for there went virtue* [power] *out of him, and healed them all"* (Luke 6:19).

It also said concerning the handkerchiefs and aprons of Paul, ". . . *God wrought special miracles by the hands of Paul: So that from his body were brought unto the sick handkerchiefs or aprons, and the diseases departed from them, and the evil spirits went out of them"* (Acts 19:11,12). What caused those evil spirits to go out? The anointing!

BOTH FAITH AND THE ANOINTING ARE IMPORTANT

We said previously that you can produce the same results by faith that you can with the anointing. But there's no use being divided on the subject. We need to know about both areas— faith *and* the anointing. For example, some people who minister under the anointing know nothing about faith. That was one of the great problems that we had way back in the days of *The Voice of Healing.*

During the great healing revival here in America from 1947 through 1958, most all the ministers were ministering under the anointing, the power of God. But some of them knew very little about the Bible. They'd make some of the most asinine statements concerning the Bible you ever heard in your lifetime! Yet they knew something about ministering under the anointing.

The Voice of Healing organization always had a convention every year at Thanksgiving time. I knew the difference between ministering under the anointing and ministering by faith, and I made a certain statement to some of the brethren who were present at the Voice of Healing Convention in Philadelphia during Thanksgiving 1954.

I said to the brethren, "When all the rest of these fellows are gone and are no longer ministering, I'll still be out here." Why? Because I ministered both ways—under the anointing and by faith. I didn't base my ministry on just the anointing or on spiritual gifts. I based my ministry on the Word. And I'm still here ministering!

WHAT HAPPENS WHEN FAITH IS NOT BALANCED WITH THE POWER

Now most of those other ministers ministered under the anointing. Some of them were used mightily by God. I could tell you about some of the mightiest miracles I've ever seen. For example, people were raised right up from deathbeds! Marvelous things happened under these preachers' ministries.

But then some of these ministers themselves would get sick. One of them once said to me, "This anointing, this gift or ministry—whatever I've got—will work for other people, but it won't work for me."

I said, "Certainly it won't! God didn't give the ministry of the apostle to minister to the *apostle*; He gave it to minister to the

Body of Christ! You're going to have to get healed just like the rest of us do—by faith—or else do without it."

This minister's eyes got really big when I said that. He looked like he'd seen a ghost!

"Well," he answered, "I guess I'll do without it then, because I don't know anything about faith."

I said, "You ought to have been listening to some of us folks who do know something about it and are preaching and teaching it."

(I wasn't being harsh with this minister; I just wanted to get across to him the importance of basing his faith on the Word. You see, just because you're anointed to do something doesn't mean you know everything. I don't know everything, and neither do you!)

I saw preacher after preacher get sick during the days of *The Voice of Healing*. Yet they were mightily used of God to minister to others under the anointing. For example, one night in a meeting, I saw one fellow minister to five adults who were deaf and mute. They had come to the meeting from a school for the deaf. And they were all instantly healed in that meeting!

This same minister also laid his hands on a blind woman, and her eyes were instantly opened. Another person was brought to one of his meetings on a stretcher. The doctors said they couldn't do anything about the man's disease, but he was instantly healed under this man's ministry—by the healing anointing or power of God.

Yet when it came to faith, this minister didn't know a thing in the world about the Bible. He knew very little when it came to healing. I'd almost fall off my seat at times because of some of the statements this poor fellow would make about faith and healing!

You see, the anointing would come on this preacher in his services, and he'd minister under that anointing. Some of the greatest things would happen in those services. But then the anointing would lift, and this preacher was left powerless, because he didn't understand the balance of faith and power.

THERE'S POWER IN JUST A MEASURE OF THE IMMEASURABLE POWER OF GOD!

The healing anointing could manifest in a person's life and ministry, but the anointing doesn't *stay* in manifestation all the time. If it did, he'd wear out physically.

It's just like getting hold of an electric wire—you couldn't hold on to that thing forever! I've had the anointing on me so strong at times that I just shook physically; I mean, I'd literally vibrate under the power of God.

I've had the anointing on me so strong that I couldn't even see the crowd. People in the crowd many times think I'm looking straight at them. They'll think, "Brother Hagin looked right at me. He must have some message for me from the Lord." But many times, to tell the real truth about it, I don't even know they're there!

Why is that? Because when you're under the anointing, you're over in another realm, the spirit realm. The greater the anointing, the more you get over in that other realm. And when you're over in that other realm to that extent, you get more results.

That's been true in my ministry. Now I don't *stay* over there in that other realm. As I said, a person can't stay under the anointing indefinitely. He wouldn't be able to stand it.

You see, our bodies are still mortal. We couldn't stand being under that much power of God for very long. I've had to say to the Lord, "Lord, turn it off. Just turn it off. I can't stand it; I can't take anymore."

I was talking some time ago to a minister friend of mine along this very line. He said to me, "Through the years, I've always 'weaved in and out' so to speak, of that anointing. But in recent time, it has come upon me more regularly. I may just be stepping into a room in my house, and that anointing will come on me. Sometimes it's so strong, I can hardly stand it. I have to say, 'Lord, turn it off. I can't take anymore.'"

I know exactly what he's talking about. Physically, a person just can't take that much of the anointing, because the anointing is *power*! And that power ministered to the sick and bound can effect a healing and a cure and bring about spectacular results to the glory of God!

—Chapter 7—

THE STRONGER
HEALING ANOINTING

Now the Bible said Jesus had the Spirit without measure (John 3:34). However, *you and I* couldn't be anointed "without measure" as Jesus was. We couldn't stand being under a strong anointing for very long.

One reason Jesus could be anointed without measure is, His body was not mortal. Now pay careful attention to what I'm saying. Yes, Jesus could be tempted in all points like we are (Heb. 4:15), because He was human, all right. But Jesus' body was like Adam's body before Adam sinned; it was neither mortal nor immortal.

Adam could be tempted. But before Adam sinned, his body was neither mortal nor immortal. Now what do I mean by that? Well, if Adam's body was mortal, it could be subject to death. But it wasn't until Adam sinned and died *spiritually* that his body became subject to physical death, and he eventually died *physically*.

ROMANS 5:12
12 Wherefore, as by one man sin entered into the world, and DEATH BY SIN; and SO DEATH PASSED UPON ALL MEN, for that all have sinned.

So mortality didn't pass upon Adam until he sinned. But on the other hand, even before Adam sinned, he did need to sustain his human body by eating. That's why the Bible said Adam could eat of certain trees and certain fruits.

Jesus had to eat to sustain Himself too. Yes, He laid aside His mighty power and glory when He came to the earth and became a man, but Jesus had the same kind of body Adam had before Adam sinned. It was neither mortal nor immortal.

That's the reason Jesus' enemies couldn't kill Jesus. They couldn't kill Jesus until He was made sin (2 Cor. 5:21). In Jesus' earth walk before the experience in the Garden of Gethsemane, whenever Jesus' enemies would try to kill Him, He'd just slip out of their midst.

LUKE 4:29-30
29 And [those in the synagogue] rose up, and thrust him [Jesus] out of the city, and led him unto the brow of the hill whereon their city was built, that they might cast him down headlong.
30 But he PASSING THROUGH THE MIDST OF THEM WENT HIS WAY.

But then in the Garden of Gethsemane when Jesus took upon Himself—His spirit nature—our sins and our diseases, then His body became mortal, and His enemies could kill Him.

You understand, of course, that they *didn't* kill Jesus! Jesus Himself said, *"No man taketh it* [my life] *from me, but I lay it down of myself. I have power to lay it down, and I have power to take it again"* (John 10:18). So they didn't kill Jesus, Jesus laid down His own life.

Can you understand the fact that before Jesus was made sin for us, He was neither mortal nor immortal? So in Jesus' earthly ministry, He could have the Spirit or power without measure—because His body was not yet subject to mortality!

Now we said before that electricity is God's power in the natural realm. Well, physically, you could stand a little bit of electricity. You could get a little bit of a shock and just shake it off; it wouldn't affect you much.

But, on the other hand, if you got hold of a lamp that had a short in it, for example, and about 110 volts hit you, you'd jump and holler! You couldn't just stand there all day and hold on to that lamp. In fact, just 110 volts could kill someone under certain circumstances. And then, of course, if someone got hold of 220 volts or more of electricity, he'd be in real trouble!

So imagine Jesus' having that Holy Spirit power without measure. It could just flow through Him and not bother Him particularly or affect Him.

THE STRONGER HEALING ANOINTING IN MY OWN MINISTRY

I know when the anointing comes on me really strong, I feel as if I'm going to fall down sometimes. At times it seems as if my legs are going to go out from under me. My hands and arms tingle. Sometimes my whole body tingles. As I said, when the healing anointing is in the palms of my hands, my hands will burn like fire.

Well, I can only stand so much of the anointing or power of God. I couldn't stand being under that power for very long. And I have just a measure of it.

Now after the Lord appeared to me in September 1950 and gave me a special anointing to minister to the sick, I began to minister with that anointing. I ministered that way through the rest of 1950 and the whole year of 1951.

Then in January 1952 I was holding a meeting in Port Arthur, Texas, in the old First Assembly of God church there. And in those days, after I preached, I gave the altar call and sent people back to the prayer room to be saved. Then I'd put the rest of the people in the same line (I called it a prayer line) to be healed and to be filled with the Holy Ghost.

In those days, I would often sit in a chair on the platform and lay hands on the people as they went by. Usually I'd talk to each person individually and spend some time with each one, because I didn't have that many people in those days to minister to—maybe twenty-five to fifty a night.

So I was sitting in a chair ministering in that meeting in Port Arthur when suddenly a stronger anointing came on me.

THE ANOINTING THAT COMES UPON A PERSON IS MEASURABLE

Now we've already seen that one can be *more* anointed or one can be *less* anointed to minister healing, preach the Gospel, or stand in any office to do anything. For example, Elisha had a double portion of the Spirit that was upon Elijah (2 Kings 2:9).

While I'm on the subject, let me clarify something concerning the anointing. When we talk about the double portion, we're talking about the anointing for ministry or the anointing *upon* a person. We can see in the case of Elijah and Elisha that Elisha was anointed with a double portion to do the work of the ministry—to be God's prophet in Israel in the place of Elijah. And there were twice as many miracles under Elisha's ministry than under Elijah's ministry (*see* 2 Kings chapters 2–13).

Yet when it comes to the born-again, Spirit-filled believer, every one of us has a measure of the Spirit *within* us, an anointing (1 John 2:27). But that anointing is different than the anointing for ministry. The anointing for ministry can be increased, but the anointing that's within every believer will never be increased.

Through the anointing that's within every believer, you can learn to walk with the Holy Spirit and know more about Him. He's there in your spirit for a certain purpose. One purpose is to teach you. Yet there's nothing in the Scripture that says you can have a double portion of that anointing.

But when it comes to the anointing to minister, one *can* have a double portion of that anointing. That anointing is the anointing that comes *upon* a person for ministry, and he or she can be more anointed or less anointed with that anointing.

THE ANOINTING UPON A PERSON IS LIKE A MANTLE OR CLOAK

As I said, I had already been ministering to the sick with the special anointing when, suddenly, in that meeting in Port Arthur, a stronger anointing came on me. I was just sitting there on the platform on a folding chair ministering to folks when it came on me in a stronger measure.

The people in the prayer line were walking in front of where I was seated, and I was laying hands on them and ministering to them. Suddenly, it felt as if somebody passed by me and threw a coat on me. It was that stronger anointing. It was just like someone in the spirit realm threw something over me. I could feel it over my whole being. It was like a cloak, and that anointing vibrated through every part of me.

I don't know how I knew it, but somehow I knew that this stronger anointing wouldn't last long. I sure didn't know that in my noggin! I just knew it in my spirit.

Why wouldn't it last long? Well, the main reason was, I couldn't have physically stood it for very long.

So knowing in my spirit that the anointing wouldn't last long, I stood up. I didn't even use the steps to come down off the platform; I just leaped off the platform and began to run.

I was so overwhelmed by the Spirit that I couldn't tell you firsthand exactly what happened. I had to depend on the pastor to tell me later what happened. All I know is, I just started running and touching people on the forehead.

Then I remember the anointing got even *stronger*. As I was running, I couldn't really see anything. (I'm not sure how to explain it. Spiritual things are difficult sometimes to "bring over" into the natural realm and explain.) I had my eyes wide open and yet I could hardly see anything.

Before that night, only a time or two did anybody ever fall under the power when I laid hands on him. But this time, everybody I touched fell! Now I say they fell, because the pastor told me later that they did.

Then suddenly that anointing lifted from me. I mean, it was just exactly as if you'd helped someone take off his coat. It just lifted, and it was gone!

Well, when the stronger anointing left, I could see everybody again. I looked around and saw all these people lying on the floor. I didn't take time to count them. I just got back up on the platform, sat down in the chair, and finished out my prayer and healing line with what I call the ordinary healing anointing.

The pastor asked me later, "Do you know how many people you touched when you were running?"

"No," I said.

"About thirty-four," he said, "and about half of them had come to receive the Holy Ghost. After you laid hands on them, they fell on the floor under the power of God, and they lay there just talking in tongues!"

The pastor continued, "Most of them are members of my church. Some of them had been seeking the baptism of the Holy Ghost for years.

"That just astounds me," he added. "I've never seen anything like it!"

Those people who'd been seeking the baptism were chronic seekers (they didn't *have* to seek the baptism in the Holy Spirit; the baptism in the Holy Spirit is a Bible promise that can simply be received and acted upon). But instantly, through the anointing, they were baptized in the Holy Ghost and spoke in tongues.

That happened in January 1952. I ministered in other meetings through the rest of 1952, the entire year of 1953, and through August 1954, and that never happened again.

Well, I didn't know whether it was *ever* going to happen again or not. God didn't tell me in the Word that it was going to happen, and I couldn't believe for something that He didn't promise me. All I could do was pray and prepare myself and do my best in believing God according to His Word. Yet, all that time, from January 1952 to August 1954, I laid hands on people constantly in my meetings and saw many healed.

Then in September 1954 I was preaching a one-day meeting in the First Foursquare Church in San Jose, California. I preached Sunday morning, Sunday afternoon, and Sunday night.

Sunday morning after I preached, I just dismissed the people afterward. I didn't take time to minister by the laying on of hands. I just said to the congregation, "You come back this afternoon and we'll lay hands on believers to be filled with the Holy Ghost, and we'll lay hands on the sick to be healed."

So I preached in the afternoon service and then had folks to come to the prayer line. I had folks who wanted to be filled with the Holy Ghost stand on one side, and two or three rows of people came to be filled with the Holy Ghost. Then I had a separate line of people who came for healing.

I started down the line praying for folks, laying hands on them, when suddenly that stronger anointing came on me again. It was like somebody ran past me and threw a cloak over me.

I could feel it all over me, and again, I knew it wouldn't last long. Why wouldn't it? Because physically, I wouldn't be able stand it.

And so when that stronger anointing came on me again, I started running, and I just touched people with my finger. I didn't take time to touch them with my hand. And everybody I touched just fell under the power of God.

To tell you the truth about it, I was caught up in the glory—in the Spirit. I don't really know everything that happened. But folks told me later that everybody I touched fell.

Then that anointing just lifted from me. I couldn't stand it any longer, and it lifted from me.

Now from 1952 to 1970, that stronger anointing came on me about four times. Then in September 1970, my wife and I were ministering in Buffalo, New York. As we were praying one day, the Lord said to me, "Have a healing seminar when you go back to Tulsa." We already had offices located there in another minister's old office building.

A New Beginning in My Ministry

We had a little chapel in that office building. It would only seat three hundred people, but you could crowd six hundred people or more in there if you had them sit real close to each other. We'd have a seminar in that chapel every so often.

The Lord told me to have a healing seminar in October in that chapel. He told me to have meetings in the evenings and on Sunday afternoon so it wouldn't conflict with church services in the city.

The Lord also told me to have a prayer seminar during the day on Monday through Friday and to teach on intercessory prayer. Those messages I taught became the book *The Interceding Christian*.

The Lord told me to begin Sunday afternoon, teaching on "Healing in the Atonement." He wanted me to teach about the redemptive plan of God that belongs to everybody. A person can just claim his healing by faith, just as he does his salvation in the New Birth. Anybody can do that at any time.

Then on Monday and Tuesday nights, I was to teach on different avenues of healing or different ways to be healed. And on Wednesday night, I was to teach on special ministries and anointings. The Lord also told me to relate my experience of twenty years before, when He first appeared to me in Rockwall, Texas, and gave me a special anointing to minister to the sick.

The Lord said, "Then after you give your experience, lay hands on the people, and that stronger anointing that has come on you four times in the last twenty years will come on you to abide."

Now that didn't mean it would be in *manifestation* all the time. It just meant that the stronger anointing would manifest regularly in my meetings instead of once every four or five years.

The Lord also said to me, "This will be a new beginning for you." And it *was* a new beginning for me.

After that, about six weeks before I was to hold another meeting, I had a vision of the meeting. In the vision, I saw people lying all over the front of the church and on the platform under the power of God.

Well, I knew what was going to happen in that meeting six weeks ahead of time, but I didn't tell anybody. I never told a soul because I didn't want anyone to think that what would happen was something psychological or something I just tried to "put on."

When it came time for that meeting, I preached and began to lay hands on the people in the prayer line. And sure enough, as I laid hands on them under that anointing, they just started falling everywhere.

EFFECTS OF THE STRONGER ANOINTING ON THE NATURAL MAN

Now the anointing on me was so strong in that meeting that when the meeting was over, I couldn't drive my car home. I couldn't even get to my car! Somebody had to lead me; I was wobbling like a drunk man!

Some people in the church drove me home and helped me out of the car. They took me inside and put me in a big chair. It was two hours before I finally got back to normal and could get out of that chair and walk!

That's one reason that during healing crusades, I leave after the meeting and get away from the crowd; that anointing seems to settle down in my legs and, often, I can't walk for a period of time.

Also, when I'm ministering under that anointing, I'll sometimes instruct people not to try to talk to me.

The reason I tell people not to try to talk to me is, if I get back over in the natural, mental realm, I'll lose the anointing. When I'm under that strong anointing, anything a person does that would bring me back into the physical, natural realm, will cause me to lose the anointing.

As I said, some of the most amazing things have happened in my ministry when I was under the anointing. And sometimes funny things happen too! For example, years ago in one of my services, I ministered to a lady in the healing line who had on a wig. Wigs were very popular then; many ladies wore them.

Well, when I laid hands on her, she went down under the power of God, and that wig fell off and landed right beside her head! I didn't even know about it until later when some folks in the group that traveled with me told me about it. They told me it looked like she had two heads!

When things like that happen, I'm not usually aware of it. But members of the singing group that travel with me during crusades are always telling me funny things that happen when I'm under that anointing. They get to laughing at me, but they always tell me what happened later—after the anointing has lifted—because if I began laughing with them at the time, I'd lose the anointing by getting back over in the natural.

Now the Lord had said to me in 1970, "That anointing will come upon you to abide." Potentially, the anointing is there all the time, but when it's in manifestation, it can be greater or lesser. As I said, the anointing was so great in the meeting the Lord had shown me in the vision that it took me two hours to get back into the natural realm.

Now I don't know if you've had any experience in the Spirit or not, but I've had a lot of experience. And I'll be perfectly honest with you, when that anointing comes upon you, from the natural standpoint, you almost could become afraid. Why? Because you're afraid you can't get back into the natural realm.

The anointing came on me so strong in one particular service, I couldn't say a word in English, and I couldn't get back into the natural for some time. I believe I know exactly what happened to Enoch in Genesis 5:24 where it said, *"And Enoch walked with God: and he was not; for God took him."* Enoch got out in the realm of the Spirit, and he couldn't get back!

Once in a meeting when I got out there in the Spirit, I kept thinking, "I'm not going to get back. I'm so far out, I can't get back!"

I always wanted to get back, so I didn't want to get out there too far. You know, a person could get out so far in the spirit realm or in the heavenly realm, that he doesn't mind going there to stay.

EXPLORING THE REALM OF THE SPIRIT

I'll tell you the truth about the matter, we are exploring the realm of the Spirit and learning some things today that we should have known yesterday.

In modern times, men have ventured into space to explore it. Yet they didn't just go to the moon the first time they ventured out into space. They barely got up in space—just so many miles up— the first time. They barely got out of the hold of gravity and over into the realm we call space.

Now why? Because they didn't know what was out there. They didn't know the rules and laws that regulated that realm. They didn't know whether or not they could get back! So they just barely went out and explored. Then the next time they went a little farther out. And then finally, they just went all the way to the moon and walked on it.

There's a parallel here between the increase in this *natural* knowledge and the increase of *spiritual* knowledge. Daniel prophesied years ago about the increase of knowledge in the last days.

DANIEL 11:32

32 And such as do wickedly against the covenant shall he corrupt by flatteries: but the people THAT DO KNOW THEIR GOD shall be strong, and DO EXPLOITS.

DANIEL 12:4

4   But thou, O Daniel, shut up the words, and seal the book, even to the time of the end: many shall run to and fro, and KNOWLEDGE SHALL BE INCREASED.

Well, knowledge has been increased. And spiritually, some of us have been going out a little bit into the edge of the Spirit. Other folks have been baptized in the Holy Ghost and have spoken with tongues. They've gotten their toes wet, so to speak, and have thought, "This is it!"

But, no, that isn't *it*. In other words, that isn't all there is to learning about the Spirit and the realm of the Spirit. Some of us have gotten out there a little further than others, but we still don't get out too far. I mean, if we do, how are we going to get back?

Now referring to our analogy of exploring space in the natural, while scientists and astronomers are doing exploits out in space, we're going to be doing exploits in the Spirit! We're going to send out Spirit-men and Spirit-women to do exploits!

Jesus hasn't changed today. He is still in the healing business. Jesus the Head of the Church is still distributing gifts and anointings, and His Word is and will always be true.

There is a healing anointing we can learn to tap into. We've got some more studying and learning to do in this area of the healing anointing, but we're not a half-step away from experiencing more of this anointing and even greater manifestations of the Spirit!

—Chapter 8—

RESULTS OF THE HEALING ANOINTING

. . . and the yoke shall be destroyed because of the anointing.

—Isaiah 10:27

In studying about the yoke-destroying anointing or the healing power, one great fact that we have established is that the healing power of God is a tangible substance, a heavenly materiality. We need to know and believe that!

John Lake was a man who was mightily used of God. He said some very interesting things about the healing power of God, including the following commentary.

> It is one of the most difficult things in all the world for people who are not familiar with the ministry of healing to comprehend that the Spirit [the anointing] of God is tangible, actual, a living quantity, just as real as electricity, just as real as any other native force. Yea and a great deal more so. The life principle that stands behind all manifestations of life everywhere.[1]

Dr. Lake went on to say the following:

> If we could make the world understand the pregnant vitality [of the power] of the Spirit of God, men would discover that healing is not only a matter of faith, and a matter of the Grace of God, but a perfectly scientific application of God's Spirit to man's needs.[2]

Another fact about the healing power of God is that it is transferable or transmittable. It can be transmitted from one to another either by the laying on of hands or by a cloth or a handkerchief, as in the clothes of Jesus and the handkerchiefs of Paul. In each case, the cloths became storage batteries, so to speak, of the healing power.

We need to thoroughly understand these aspects of the healing anointing so we can make the anointing useful to our lives. We need to know the laws or rules that govern the healing power so we can obtain the results or benefits of the anointing. That's why we keep going over it.

It's sort of like eating a good meal. For example, I like T-bone steaks, but I don't say, "Well, I just had a steak last week. I don't believe I'll have another one." No, I eat steaks every chance I get!

And, you know, this subject of the healing anointing is good eating! The Word of God is good eating! I get blessed by it over and over again.

OTHER RESULTS OF THE ANOINTING

We talked about some of the effects of the healing anointing—the special anointing that God anoints certain individuals with to minister to the sick. We looked at many cases of healing in the Bible under the ministries of Jesus and Paul. We also looked at cases of healing under my own ministry and the ministries of other modern-day preachers.

But the healing anointing doesn't just work to drive out sickness and disease. Our text said, ". . . *the YOKE shall be destroyed because of the anointing*" (Isa. 10:27). Remember we said in previous chapters that a yoke is anything that holds a person in bondage. A person could be in bondage to or held captive by any number of things, not just sickness and disease.

THE SPECIAL ANOINTING ALSO DRIVES OUT EVIL SPIRITS

I alluded to it earlier, but now I'll go into more detail about another fact that we haven't always seen about the healing anointing. This is the fact: The healing anointing will not only drive out sickness and disease, but it will drive out evil spirits too.

LUKE 6:17–19

17 And he [Jesus] came down with them, and stood in the plain, and the company of his disciples, and a great multitude of people out of all Judaea and Jerusalem, and from the sea coast of Tyre and Sidon, which came to hear him, and to be healed of their diseases;

18 And THEY THAT WERE VEXED WITH UNCLEAN SPIRITS: and they WERE HEALED.

19 And the whole multitude sought to touch him: FOR THERE WENT VIRTUE [power] out of him, and healed them all.

Verses 17 and 18 say that both those who were diseased and those who were vexed with unclean spirits were *healed*. How were they healed? Verse 19 says ". . . *for there went VIRTUE* [power] *out of him, and healed them all.*"

Then in Matthew chapter 8, it says that Jesus "cast out the spirits with His Word, and healed all that were sick."

MATTHEW 8:16

16 When the even was come, they brought unto him many that were possessed with devils: and HE CAST OUT THE SPIRITS WITH HIS WORD, and HEALED ALL THAT WERE SICK.

Now this scripture doesn't say how the sick were healed; it just says they were healed. Jesus could have healed the sick with or without the healing anointing, but He cast out the spirits with His Word. Concerning those who were demon possessed, it says, ". . . *he* [Jesus] *cast out the spirits with his word . . . ."*

So we see in Matthew 8:16 the connection between *healing* and *deliverance from evil spirits.*

But notice again the passage of scripture in Luke 6:17–19. Verse 18 says, *"And they that were vexed with unclean spirits: and they were healed."* Evidently, in this case, those who were vexed with unclean spirits were healed by the healing anointing, because verse 19 says, *"And the whole multitude sought to TOUCH him: for there went VIRTUE out of him, and HEALED THEM ALL."*

But over in Matthew 8:16 it says, ". . . *he cast out the spirits WITH HIS WORD."*

Somebody said, "Evil spirits always have to be *cast* out." But, no. That's where people miss it sometimes. Certainly, you can speak the Word of faith to cast evil spirits out. But when you're operating under the *anointing,* the anointing will *drive* them out!

Go back again to Acts 19:11 and 12.

ACTS 19:11–12

11 And God wrought special miracles by the hands of Paul:

12 So that from his body were brought unto the sick handkerchiefs or aprons, and the DISEASES DEPARTED FROM THEM, and the EVIL SPIRITS WENT OUT OF THEM.

Verse 12 says that evil spirits went out of folks when those cloths touched them. It wasn't a matter of somebody discerning the evil spirits, and it wasn't a matter of somebody speaking the Word and casting them out. It was a matter of the anointing *driving* them out!

LEARN HOW GOD WORKS AND WORK WITH HIM

You see, our problem many times is that we want to put everything in a little box, so to speak, and have the attitude *That's it; there's only one way to do this.*

Many times in our narrow thinking, we do not allow God to do everything He wants to do, because we imagine that whatever God does has to be done some certain way and that's it—there's no other way.

Some people believe that devils or demons always have to be discerned and cast out. But, no, we just read that when the handkerchiefs of Paul were laid on the sick, diseases departed from them and the evil spirits went out of them (Acts 19:12). The evil spirits that left those folks were not discerned *or* cast out! The Bible just says that when the handkerchiefs or cloths were laid on the sick, the diseases departed from the sick and the evil spirits went out of them too.

You see, the same anointing that's ministered to folks for healing will drive out evil spirits too.

People will often come up to me after they've been prayed for in a healing line, and they'll say, "I went into the prayer line for healing. I thought I had faith for healing, but then I got to thinking that maybe I had a devil."

I always say to them, "What difference does it make? The same power that drives out sickness drives out devils, and that power went into you. So forget about whether or not you have a devil, and just go on in faith. You're delivered."

"Yes," they'll say, "but I thought a devil had to be *discerned*" or "I thought a devil had to be *cast out*."

That's the trouble. People go by what they *think* instead of what the Bible said!

A Power Greater Than Any Yoke!

Now if you're operating in faith without the anointing, you *do* have to speak the Word in faith. But when the healing anointing is in manifestation, the same anointing that drives out sickness and disease can drive out evil spirits too!

Notice the Bible doesn't say anything about Paul speaking any Word when those handkerchiefs were laid on folks

(Acts 19:11–12). And it doesn't say anything about Jesus speaking any Word in Luke chapter 6.

LUKE 6:17–19

17 And he came down with them, and stood in the plain, and the company of his disciples, and a great multitude of people out of all Judaea and Jerusalem, and from the sea coast of Tyre and Sidon, which came to hear him, and to be healed of their diseases;

18 And they that were vexed with unclean spirits: and they were healed.

19 And the whole multitude sought to touch him: for there went virtue out of him, and healed THEM ALL.

Who are the "them all" in verse 19? That's the "them all" who had diseases (v. 17) and the "them all" who were vexed with unclean spirits (v. 18)! The anointing drives out sickness and disease *and* evil spirits!

I noticed that in my own ministry. People would come into my healing lines for healing, but under the tangible healing anointing, they received more than healing. Many of them who needed deliverance from evil spirits received deliverance too.

I have dealt with people who in times past were mixed up with the occult. Then they got born again and Spirit-filled, and they began living right; yet they still experienced manifestations of evil spirits.

The evil spirits kept manifesting themselves in those people's lives. No, the evil spirits weren't *in* those Christians; but they were *around* them, harassing them. For example, the people would hear rappings on the wall and voices in the nighttime.

But these same people would get in the healing line for healing, and they would receive deliverance too!

I've had a number of folks come up for prayer who were bound with alcohol. Some of them would come for prayer for that very purpose—to be delivered from alcoholism. Others came for healing.

I've had any number of testimonies from people who received deliverance from evil spirits through the anointing. They'd say to me, "Brother Hagin, when you laid hands on me in the healing line, I'd been bound with alcohol twenty-five years. But I was set free by the power of God!"

One fellow who'd been an officer in the United States Army testified to me about a year after he'd been delivered from alcoholism. He said, "When I was in the military, I went into three different government hospitals to take the cure for alcoholism. But I came out of those hospitals drinking."

After he got out of the service, he put himself in three more different hospitals, and he still came out drinking.

Of course, this man had been away from God all those years. But he said he remembered back when he was thirteen years old, at a time when he knew the Lord. He said, "I remembered the story of the prodigal son [Luke 15:11-24]. So I just got down on my knees and prayed, 'Dear Lord, I'm coming home like the prodigal son of old. I ask You to forgive me.'"

This man said, "I know the Lord took me back. I had peace in my spirit. It felt to me just like a two thousand-pound weight rolled off of my chest. But my body was still bound with that alcohol demon. I couldn't quit drinking."

He related: "One of my friends said to me, 'Why don't you go out to this meeting I've been going to?'" (It was a meeting I was holding.)

So this retired Army officer came to my meeting. What he saw there was all new to him. He later said, "I didn't understand a thing that was going on. Of course, I hadn't been in church for years, so I didn't know anything about the laying on of hands and about everybody lifting their hands and praying at once out loud." You see, back when he had gone to church as a boy, the church he went to was quiet.

He said to me, "Nearly everybody you laid hands on fell on the floor, and that startled me." But then he said to his friend who had invited him to the meeting, "I'm going down there to be prayed for because I desperately need help. But I'm not going to fall down like the rest of them."

The Army officer continued, "After I went down to get in the healing line and you laid hands on me, the next thing I knew, I was getting up off the floor. I don't even remember falling."

He said, "Two outstanding things happened to me when you laid hands on me and that power came all over me. It was sort of like electricity, and a warmth went all over me.

"First, I had a great spiritual experience. I got closer to Jesus. It brought me closer to Him and made me love Him more. Second, that alcohol demon I was bound with all those years left me. I've never touched another drop of alcohol since. I've never even *wanted* another drink."

Thank God for the power of God—the anointing!

The Bible says, *"the diseases departed from them, and the evil spirits went out of them"* (Acts 19:12)! There is a power that's greater than the power of the devil. There is a power that's greater than sickness and disease. It is the power of God!

You Must Know Something Exists to Benefit From It

We're talking about the results of the healing anointing—of the mighty healing power of God. Why haven't we seen more results of the healing anointing? Part of the reason is that many people haven't known that the power even existed. And then some of those who knew it existed haven't known how to tap into the power and get it to produce any results.

As I already stated, there is a parallel between electricity in the natural realm and God's power in the supernatural realm. And just as man discovered the laws that governed the operation of electricity, we can discover and put to use the laws that govern the operation of the *heavenly* electricity, the power of God.

We know that electricity was in existence from the time God created the universe. Well, since electricity was in existence since the beginning of creation, why didn't it just automatically operate or manifest itself? Because certain laws govern the operation of electricity.

People ask that same question about the heavenly electricity—the anointing: "If the power of God is always present, why doesn't it just manifest itself? It must not really be present. Or maybe it doesn't really exist."

But the power of God is real, and it is present everywhere. Most people just don't know the spiritual laws that govern its operation.

PUTTING DISCOVERIES TO USE

In the natural, man had to first *discover* electricity before he could begin to explore ways to make electricity operate and benefit man. You see, just because you don't *know* something exists doesn't mean it doesn't really exist. It just means you don't know about it. Therefore, you couldn't benefit from it. But when you know that something exists, such as electricity or the power of God, you are in a position to benefit from its existence.

For example, think about the years gone by before man knew electricity existed. Men lived in caves and didn't have any light or fire. Finally, they discovered how to make fire, but they didn't benefit from electricity.

Even when people discovered that electricity existed, they didn't know how to put it to work for them. Then in more modern times, Benjamin Franklin discovered how to harness electricity to make it useful. He learned how to put it to work, and what a blessing electricity has been to mankind since that time!

The Blessing Comes When the Power Is Put Into Action

Man has benefited greatly from the discovery of electricity by learning how to put it to use. In fact, we just take electricity for granted today until something happens to stop the flow of electricity in our homes and so forth.

We don't realize what a blessing electricity is until a storm comes along and blows down the power lines. Then our refrigerators and freezers don't run, and our frozen meats and vegetables are ruined. And the air conditioners and heaters won't work, and it gets either too hot or too cold inside.

Some of us are old enough to remember many years ago when we didn't have any of these appliances. They hadn't been invented.

I can remember when I was a little kid, we didn't have any electric refrigerators. We had iceboxes. A fellow would come around the neighborhoods delivering ice to put in the iceboxes to keep them cold. He pulled his ice wagon with a horse (later, he did get a Model-T Ford in place of his horse and wagon).

But when refrigerators were invented, one by one, people began getting refrigerators. When my wife and I first married, we just had an icebox. We were pastoring our second church before we ever got a refrigerator, and that was after Ken and Pat were born. Man alive, we thought we were in Heaven, so to speak, when we got that refrigerator! We were benefiting to a greater degree from the power of electricity.

When we pastored our second church, we also didn't have running water in the house. We had a path instead of a bath! (Young people nowadays have it easy compared to when we were young.)

We didn't have running water in the third church we pastored either. Of course, that meant there was no water in the kitchen. You had to carry water in a bucket.

In the fourth church we pastored, we still didn't have running water in the house. That was in 1943. We did have a hydrant out in the yard though that we used to fill up our buckets.

Finally I said, "I know what I'm going to do." You see, I'd learned a little bit through the years about plumbing and electrical work because I'd helped a fellow build some houses. I also learned a little bit about carpentry work, and I learned to paint and wallpaper. So I said, "I'm going to run a water line from that hydrant into the house."

The hydrant was about fifteen feet from the kitchen window. It would be a very easy matter just to dig a little trench from the hydrant to the kitchen and then put in fifteen feet of pipe and a riser to bring the water inside the house.

I needed to have a cabinet built under the sink, so I found a preacher who was a cabinet maker and was also full of wisdom and the Holy Ghost. I got him to preach at night and build me a cabinet in the daytime!

This minister put in a beautiful cabinet, and we had running water indoors! We didn't have *hot* water; we still had to heat our water in a tea kettle on the stove. But we had running water!

Then some folks in the church got mad and griped about that, saying, "Well, I don't have running water in *my* house!"

My answer was, "If you weren't so lazy, you could!"

I didn't ask anybody to install those pipes for me; I just dug that ditch myself, plus I did all the plumbing. I could have built the cabinet myself, too, but that was this other minister's area of expertise. He was an expert carpenter. Any cabinet I would have built would have looked like it belonged in a barn rather than in a house!

So then we had a refrigerator and running water indoors in our three-room parsonage. We thought we had "arrived"! We thought surely it couldn't get any better than this!

But then in that same parsonage, we just had a wood stove to heat the whole house with. Actually, you could heat the living room, but the bedroom was cold.

In the kitchen, there was an old kerosene cook stove. But in 1943, during World War II, you couldn't buy spare parts for the thing. So all our food smelled like kerosene or coal oil.

Finally, I said, "You know, I believe I'll just put a gas stove in here." After all, we'd had a gas stove in the parsonage where we'd lived before. I owned the open heaters and the gas cook stove, but I couldn't use them in our new parsonage because there was nothing to hook them up to; there was no gas line that ran into the house.

Well, because the war was on, you couldn't get pipe-to-pipe gas up to your property, and you couldn't buy pipe without a "priority" permit. So I had to go to the gas company and fill out a whole list of paperwork.

The gas company wanted to know where you came from, who your grandma and great-grandma were—*and* your grandpa, cousin, uncle, and aunt! They wanted to know how old you were, how long you expected to live, and how much you weighed!

I'm exaggerating, of course, but there *were* three or four forms that I had to fill out.

Finally, they asked, "What did you heat with last year?"

I told them I heated with wood and kerosene, and they told me that I didn't qualify for the priority and that I couldn't buy any pipe from them.

But later I happened to be walking by a plumbing shop, and I saw all kinds of pipe being unloaded right out on the sidewalk. I stopped and asked the plumber about it. He said, "I found this pipe in Fort Worth, and I got it without a priority. If you want it, you can buy it. But you'll just have to take what I've got."

Then a man at the gas company said, "You know, I found some pipe out behind a substation. Weeds have grown up around it, so I didn't even know we had it. I can use that pipe to finish piping gas right up to the edge of your property without any permit at all."

So I bought the pipe from the plumber. I got a young man in the church to help me, and we dug the ditch to lay the pipe in. Then the man from the gas company came with his pipe, and we hooked the pipe onto that gas line and ran the gas right into the parsonage.

Since we had a stove for every room, we had plenty of heat for the whole parsonage, plus we were able to use the gas stove instead of the kerosene stove in the kitchen.

Well, then we *knew* it couldn't get any better than that! I mean, we *really* thought we'd arrived because we had a refrigerator, running water, *and* gas heat!

Here's what I'm saying. When you don't know that something exists, you can't take advantage of it. And even when you do know that something exists, such as electricity or the power of God, you still have to know how it operates and how to tap into it in order to gain any benefit from it. But when you put it to use, what a blessing it can be!

GOD'S WORD: THE KEY TO UNDERSTANDING THE ANOINTING

When men first discovered electricity, they didn't know that it would heat, cool, and light their homes. Yet electricity could do all of those things. You see, the potential was there all the time.

If somebody would have told some caveman and cavewoman, "Boy, you ought to wire your cave for electricity," they'd ask, "What's 'electricity'?"

"Oh, you know, it's power, and it flows through wires."

The caveman would say, "What are wires?"

Then later, after the person finished telling the caveman and cavewoman all about electricity, that caveman would probably say to his wife, "That fellow ought to be put away—he's crazy! We know that nothing like that even exists!"

That's similar to trying to explain the power of God to some church people who don't know a thing about it. They've never heard about it, and if they've read the Bible, they just simply read over the "power" part, wearing glasses colored with tradition. They would say, "Those folks who believe in that power business have gone 'off their rockers.' We know the power of God doesn't exist, because if it did, we'd have it."

Bless their darlin' hearts and stupid heads! They missed it. They've just never taken time to get into the Book to find out what was in there. They just imagined God operates a certain way, and that's it—there's nothing more to learn. They imagined that if the power of God were real, it would just manifest. So if it didn't manifest, they thought that the power wasn't real or that it wasn't present.

Then on the other hand, many have known that the healing power of God does exist. Some have even come in contact with it, yet they haven't necessarily understood how to put it to work. But, thank God, we have the Word to help us understand how to put the power to work!

Even Medical Science Has Recognized the Anointing

I read an article in a secular magazine that was written in conjunction with three medical doctors who were scientists. They said, "We have run through the laboratory all the old Indian remedies that we could find."

The doctors continued, "We, being men of science, didn't think any of those remedies would work. But we found that nearly all of them did. And we found out why.

"We discovered that certain weeds, roots and other things that the Indians used for cures contained some of the very medicines we use in medical science today.

"Then we took all the old wives' cures and folklore remedies we could find and tested them too. And to our utter astonishment, we found that the majority of them worked on the very ailments people claimed they would work on."

In recent times, I read in the newspaper that another group of medical scientists said, "We don't know why it works, but we've discovered that 'Grandma' was right—if you've got a cold, eat chicken soup!"

You see, medical science has never found a cure for the common cold. But these scientists said they'd found that chicken soup was one of the greatest aids in fighting the common cold that they knew about.

Well, "Grandma" knew that. Chicken soup was the first thing she'd give you when you got sick with a cold.

Those three doctors who wrote the magazine article said, "We're in the healing business, so we haven't got a right to withhold any kind of healing from people. If it's Indian remedies that work, fine. If it's old wives' tales that work, fine."

Then they said, "We've even found that divine healing works." (That's what they called it—divine healing.) They said, "We've proven that it works."

These doctors continued: "If we could run divine healing through the laboratory, we could find out *how* it works."

You see, they could run the other remedies through their labs and find out what ingredients were in them. They knew there had to be something in those remedies that fought certain fevers or diseases. And by running them through the lab, they found out what it was.

But you can't run divine healing through a laboratory or look at it under a microscope. The doctors said, "We've got the proof that divine healing works; we have the scientific facts. We've got it all down in writing. We just don't know *how* it works."

These doctors wrote about a man in the hospital whom medical science had given up to die. The man had terminal cancer. They put it this way: "A man of the cloth came in and anointed him with oil and laid hands on him. And in three days the cancer patient was well."

Then they cited a number of other cases that they had documented. These doctors knew about some of the *results* of the anointing, but they didn't know how to *obtain* or *produce* the results of the anointing.

They testified, "Divine healing works. If we knew how to make it work, we'd take divine healing to people. But we don't know how to make it work."

As I read that, I thought, *I know exactly how to make it work!*

THE WORD OF GOD IS A 'MICROSCOPE'

No, you can't look at divine healing and the healing power of God through a microscope, and you can't run it through a laboratory to find out what makes it work. But, blessed be God, you *can* look at divine healing in the Word of God and find your answer! Faith makes divine healing work. Faith activates the power!

Jesus said to the woman with the issue of blood, "Daughter, thy *faith* hath made thee whole" (Mark 5:34). *Faith* is what makes the power work.

"Oh, I don't believe in that faith-healing business or in those faith healers," some say.

I used to almost resent it in times gone by when people, even other ministers, called some of us preachers "faith healers."

Those people thought they were doing us an injustice by calling us "faith healers," and we sort of felt that way too. But I got to studying the Bible, and I finally just became proud of the fact they called us faith healers. I mean, who would object to being classed along with Jesus? Jesus was a Man of faith. He was the One—it wasn't me—who said, *"Therefore I say unto you, What things soever ye desire, when ye pray, believe that ye receive them, and ye shall have them"* (Mark 11:24).

Jesus said, *"Daughter, thy FAITH hath made thee whole"* (Mark 5:34). Jesus Himself was a faith Teacher and a faith Preacher, so to make fun of "faith healing" is to make fun of Jesus.

Well, who would object to being accused of teaching the same things Jesus and the apostles taught? I'm in their class! You can get in whatever class you want to get in, but I'm going to stay in the class I'm in, glory to God!

Some preachers, bless their darlin' hearts, are in unbelief. Some of these fellows, if they ever had God in them, they educated Him *out*! They went to a "cemetery"—a seminary—where so-called theologians told them God was dead and that He never does anything anymore.

You can understand then why they'd make fun and say some of the things they say when they get around preachers who know something about the power of God.

I've heard such ignorant remarks made about faith and about God and His power. The people who made those remarks didn't realize they were talking against the Bible and criticizing their own Lord and Savior Jesus Christ. I just thought, "Bless their hearts."

Not only that, but Jesus Himself said, *"Inasmuch as ye have done it unto one of the least of these my brethren, ye have done it unto me"* (Matt. 25:40). So if a person is criticizing and talking against his brother or sister, he's really talking about Jesus. According to that scripture, Matthew 25:40, Jesus said he is.

But those people who called us "faith healers" had never matured enough or read enough to know better (they didn't call us "faith healers" as a compliment). They never looked into the microscope of God's Word by studying what *God* has to say about faith and healing and the power of God.

You could weep about it, really, you feel so sorry for folks like that. You see, spiritually speaking, many of them are in the babyhood stage.

God in His great mercy just overlooks some things when folks are in the babyhood stage of spiritual growth. And thank God, we who preach and teach faith and know something about the power of God are magnanimous enough to overlook it too!

THE CORPORATE ANOINTING

We've been talking primarily about the healing anointing or the special anointing to minister to the sick that God anoints certain individuals with. But we couldn't talk about the results of the anointing without talking about the corporate anointing.

You see, there are individual anointings, such as we've been talking about. We talked about the anointing that's within *every* believer and then about the anointing that comes only upon certain individuals as God wills. You remember we said a person couldn't anoint himself for ministry, and he can't anoint himself with the special anointing to minister to the sick. God has to do that; man can't do it himself.

So there is an individual anointing to minister to the sick. But, really, the greatest anointing of all is the corporate anointing. I can be anointed to minister to the sick and lay hands on people, and a certain percentage of them will get healed through faith and the anointing. But the corporate anointing has a greater, more far-reaching effect.[3]

So many times in meetings, we are conscious of the Presence of God's Spirit in our midst. But why doesn't He manifest Himself more often in what we call the corporate anointing?

The Scripture tells us about the singers and players of musical instruments becoming as one in singing praises to God. Then it tells about the "cloud" or the glory of God—the anointing—coming in and filling the building, so much so that the priests couldn't even stand up to minister.

You see, the Presence of God, the Holy Ghost, will manifest Himself, sometimes like a cloud. He did that in Second Chronicles 5:13 and 14. It says, *"the house was filled with a cloud, even the house of the Lord; So that the priests could not stand to minister by reason of the cloud: for the glory of the Lord had filled the house of God."*

There's something about a corporate body of believers praising God that brings forth the manifestation of His glory!

Once when I was preaching, it seemed as if a wind went through the building we were in. Everybody heard it. And every sinner in the building was saved; every backslider was rededicated; everybody who didn't have the baptism in the Holy Spirit started talking in tongues; and every sick person was healed! What happened? The corporate anointing was manifested in our midst!

I've also seen the power of God come into a meeting, and there'd be such a holy awe among the congregation. Nobody would say a word. Not a child would cry. You could have heard a pin drop.

What was that? It was a manifestation of the glory of God—the corporate anointing in the midst of a body of believers. The glory of God came in that place. It seemed as if you could have cut a chunk out of the glory to take home with you!

Several years ago when my son-in-law was my office manager, we held some radio rallies in Denver. Then we held a little three-night crusade in Longmont, Colorado.

A lady who attended the meeting with her husband wrote to me afterward. She said, "My husband claimed to be a Christian. He was a church member. I don't want to be his judge, but if he was really saved . . . well . . . there were no fruits of his salvation. He acted just like a sinner.

"He had a severe heart attack. And the heart specialist in Denver told me that they'd done all they could for him and that he had only about six months to live."

Well, this woman wanted her husband to get healed. He was only somewhere in his forties; he was not an old man.

She said, "I just nagged him and 'ding-donged' him until I got him to come to your meeting. We went on the last night of the meeting, and by the time we got there, the building was full. Finally, the usher found us two seats in the balcony. I think he got somebody else to move because of my husband's condition."

She continued: "After the meeting started, I wished we hadn't come. I almost ducked my head in shame. My husband criticized everything that went on and everything you said.

"Then you started laying hands on people, and they started falling under the power.

"My husband said, 'Aw, he's just hypnotizing them. That's all that is.'"

Now I'd had one healing line formed in that meeting and had laid hands on the people in that line. And most of them did fall under the power of God as I laid hands on them. Then, since it was our last night to be there, we formed a second line, and I continued to lay hands on people.

As I got pretty close to the pulpit, I saw this cloud—the glory of God—come in. I saw it just as plain. It looked like a white cloud or dense fog, except it came rolling in like waves of the sea.

Now when I see that cloud (I see it once in a while), I know what will happen. So as soon as I saw that cloud come rolling in over the congregation, I stopped laying hands on people. And when the cloud got right over those people in the healing line, I waved my hand, and every one of them went down like dominoes! I never touched a single one of them!

That cloud was the glory of God, the power of God! It was the same anointing in a greater measure than the measure I was anointed with. And it was the faith of the crowd that had brought that anointing in a greater measure.

Remember I said the faith of the crowd can either help or hinder the anointing. Well, overall the people were with me that night; they weren't pulling against me. They were in unity and as a result, the atmosphere became filled and charged with that power.

That woman's husband who'd been criticizing the service was sitting where the cloud had passed. The woman said, "He was just sitting there when suddenly he said, 'Oh, it's on me! It's going all over me! It's going all over me!'

"I said, 'What's going all over you?'

"He said, 'That warm glow the preacher was talking about.'"

And that man was perfectly healed, sitting up there in the balcony! He was healed by the same anointing I was anointed with, except it was a *greater* anointing. It was a corporate anointing.

This lady said in her letter, "After the meeting, my husband went right back to the same heart specialist who'd diagnosed him previously. After the examination, the doctor looked at my husband and said, 'I'll tell you one thing about it. Somebody up there likes you. You've got a brand-new heart. There's not a thing wrong with it.'"

This woman also said, "Brother Hagin, I want you to know I've got a brand-new husband." She wasn't just talking about his being brand-new *physically*. She meant she had a brand-new husband *spiritually*. Thank God for the anointing!

It's the anointing that breaks the yoke. The yoke shall be destroyed because of the anointing!

And the healing anointing is tangible. It's perceptible to the touch. You can feel or sense it, and you can receive the results of the anointing in your own life to destroy *any* yoke of bondage!

---

[1]Gordon Lindsay (ed.), *The John G. Lake Sermons on Dominion Over Demons, Disease, and Death,* Christ for the Nations, Inc., Dallas, 1979, p. 56.

[2]Ibid., p. 47.

[3]For a further study of the different kinds of anointing, *see* Rev. Hagin's book *Understanding the Anointing.*

—Chapter 9—

HOW YOU CAN RECEIVE DIVINE HEALING

. . . and the yoke shall be destroyed because of the anointing.

— Isaiah 10:27

Our golden text says, *"the yoke shall be destroyed because of the anointing."* We sometimes say it like this: "It's the anointing that destroys the yoke" or "It's the anointing that *breaks* the yoke." Well, if the anointing *destroys* the yoke, it *breaks* it!

I've been applying Isaiah 10:27 to healing because we've been talking primarily about the healing anointing. Therefore, we could say that it is the anointing that destroys or breaks the yoke of *sickness*. Thank God for the anointing!

I've also been talking about the results of the mighty healing power of God or the healing anointing. But we can't do a thorough study of the healing anointing without telling how to *obtain* the results—how to get the anointing working in your own life to produce results.

We know that in order to get the anointing to work, we've got to understand something about the operation of the anointing, and I've already discussed that. For example, we know that the anointing is *transmittable* and that it can be transmitted or transferred through certain substances, such as cloth. We also know that the anointing is *measurable* as in the case of Elijah and Elisha.

Elisha received a double portion or twice as much of the anointing that Elijah was anointed with.

We also learned that the anointing is *tangible* as illustrated in the case of the woman with the issue of blood. Jesus was aware of the *outflow* of power. He said, "Who touched My clothes?" And the woman was aware of the *inflow* of power: *". . . she FELT in her body that she was healed of that plague"* (Mark 5:29).

Well, if you can feel something, that means it's tangible. Tangible means *capable of being touched* or *perceptible to the touch.*

APPROPRIATING THE BENEFITS OF THE HEALING ANOINTING

We understand more now about the power of God or the anointing: The power is *transmittable, measurable,* and *tangible.* But to get the anointing or power to work effectually, we also have to understand the mixing of faith *with* the power so we can realize the blessings and benefits of the anointing.

You remember I said that many people have missed it because they imagined that if the tangible healing anointing is present, it will just manifest itself and do the job. But that's not necessarily true.

I also said we need to see what the *Bible* says about the healing anointing. And, of course, by looking at what the Bible says, we can't overlook the ministry of Jesus, because Jesus ministered with that anointing during His earth walk.

JESUS MINISTERED WITH AND WITHOUT THE HEALING ANOINTING

We're talking about the healing anointing, but you understand, of course, that Jesus ministered healing to people in various ways. There was not always a transfer of healing power or anointing from Him to them. Sometimes there was a transfer of power, but at other times, there wasn't.

THE CASE OF THE TEN LEPERS

For example, Jesus ministered to the ten lepers without ever touching them. No power flowed out of Jesus to the lepers. Jesus just said to them, *"Go shew yourselves unto the priests"* (Luke 17:14). And it says that as they went, they were cleansed.

THE CENTURION AND HIS SERVANT

We can also read in Matthew 8:5 and 6 about the centurion who came to Jesus on behalf of his servant. His servant had the palsy and was grievously tormented.

MATTHEW 8:5-6
5   And when Jesus was entered into Capernaum, there came unto him a centurion, beseeching him,
6   And saying, Lord, my servant lieth at home sick of the palsy, grievously tormented.

Notice how Jesus responded.

MATTHEW 8:7–10

7   And Jesus saith unto him, I will come and heal him.

8   The centurion answered and said, Lord, I am not worthy that thou shouldest come under my roof: but speak the word only, and my servant shall be healed.

9   For I am a man under authority, having soldiers under me: and I say to this man, Go, and he goeth; and to another, Come, and he cometh; and to my servant, Do this, and he doeth it.

10 When Jesus heard it, he marvelled, and said to them that followed, Verily I say unto you, I have not found so great faith, no, not in Israel.

Then verse 13 said, *"Jesus said unto the centurion, Go thy way; and as thou hast believed, so be it done unto thee. And his servant was healed in the selfsame hour."*

Well now, there wasn't any anointing that flowed from Jesus into that servant; the servant was some distance away. No, the centurion *just acted on the Word of Jesus*: "Go thy way. And as you have believed, so be it done unto you"!

You see, as we already stated, faith in God's Word works whether or not there's any tangible anointing, because the Word of God is already anointed! Jesus said, *". . . the words that I speak unto you, they are SPIRIT, and they are life"* (John 6:63).

The Bible also says about the Word, *". . . holy men of God spake as they were moved by the Holy Ghost"* (2 Peter 1:21). Holy men of old wrote as they were moved by the Holy Ghost! This Word is the *anointed* Word of God!

THE NOBLEMAN AND HIS SON

Then we read about the nobleman who came to Jesus in John chapter 4 on behalf of his son. The nobleman's son was sick and nigh unto death.

JOHN 4:50

50 Jesus saith unto him, Go thy way; thy son liveth. And the man BELIEVED the word that Jesus had spoken unto him, and he went his way.

What if this nobleman hadn't believed the word that Jesus spoke to him? Well, his son wouldn't have been healed. But the nobleman *did* believe the word which Jesus had spoken, and it said the nobleman's son was healed!

JOHN 4:51-53

51 And as he was now going down, his servants met him, and told him, saying, Thy son liveth.

52 Then inquired he of them the hour when he began to amend. And they said unto him, Yesterday at the seventh hour the fever left him.

53 So the father knew that it was at the same hour, in the which Jesus said unto him, Thy son liveth: and himself believed, and his whole house.

Now this nobleman couldn't *see* that his son "liveth," as Jesus had said, because it was sometime the following day before the man arrived back home. But the nobleman departed from Jesus, believing the words that Jesus had spoken. And when the man got home, his servants ran to meet him and said, "Thy son liveth!"

Then the nobleman asked his servants what time his son began to amend. They said, "Yesterday, about the seventh hour." That would have been at about one o'clock in the afternoon.

Well, that nobleman couldn't have had evidence that his son was healed until the day *after* Jesus spoke those words to him, *"Go thy way; thy son liveth"* (John 4:50). Why? Because he was at least a day's journey away from his son (he'd traveled that far to see Jesus).

The nobleman's son was healed, but, you see, Jesus didn't touch the man's son; He didn't lay hands on him. Therefore, we know there wasn't any transfer of power. So what happened? The nobleman just believed what Jesus said, and his son was healed!

DON'T LIMIT GOD AND MISS YOUR BLESSING!

We have to realize that there is no set way by which folks may receive healing. There are a number of methods for receiving healing recorded in the Word. And, thank God, all of them work!

In this book we're mainly emphasizing the healing anointing. But on the other hand, if you had to be ministered to by someone who was anointed with healing power, then you'd really be at a disadvantage if you were some distance away and couldn't get to that person. If that were the only way you could receive healing, you'd be at a loss.

But, thank God, you can just believe God's Word and receive healing for yourself. That's the reason we keep teaching faith!

However, everyone's not at that level. Not everyone is at the level in his faith where he can just believe God's Word for himself and receive healing according to the Word alone. Therefore, we should endeavor to teach and preach all of it—every side of divine healing—and to minister to people on all levels of faith and by all methods of healing.

So I don't want to leave the impression that ministering with the healing anointing is the only way to minister healing. I just want to make the point that it is *one* way to minister. And it is scriptural or biblical.

You can receive divine healing any number of ways. We talked about simply receiving healing by faith in the Word without any transfer of power, and we talked about receiving through the healing anointing.

But notice something in the cases I talked about in which a person was healed through the healing anointing: It wasn't the healing anointing alone that healed him or her. Something else was working with the anointing to bring about the healing. What was that something else? It was faith.

MIXING FAITH WITH THE POWER

I've already covered in detail the case of the woman with the issue of blood in Mark chapter 5. But notice the fact that she cooperated with the anointing that flowed from Jesus into her, and she was healed.

The Healing Anointing

MARK 5:27–30, 32–34

27 When she had heard of Jesus, came in the press behind, and touched his garment.

28 For she said, If I may touch but his clothes, I shall be whole.

29 And straightway the fountain of her blood was dried up; and she felt in her body that she was healed of that plague.

30 And Jesus, immediately knowing in himself that virtue [or power] had gone out of him, turned him about in the press, and said, Who touched my clothes?

32 And he looked round about to see her that had done this thing.

3 But the woman fearing and trembling, knowing what was done in her, came and fell down before him, and told him all the truth.

34 And he said unto her, Daughter, thy FAITH hath made thee whole; go in peace, and be whole of thy plague.

The healing anointing flowed out of Jesus' clothes and into the woman with the issue of blood. But Jesus said to her, "Thy *faith* hath made thee whole." It wasn't the healing anointing alone that healed this woman. It was her faith in the healing anointing that healed her. Or we could say it like this: It was her faith *and* the healing anointing that healed her.

We learned that the healing power of God or the anointing is a tangible substance. It is a heavenly materiality. Believe that, and it will work for you.

In fact, if you're going to be ministered to in this way—with the anointing—you will *have* to believe in the healing anointing, or it *won't* work for you.

HEALING AND MIRACLES DON'T AUTOMATICALLY FOLLOW THE POWER

Many people, particularly in Pentecostal circles, have thought that if the power of God was present, it's just going to manifest itself, regardless of whether or not anyone believed in it or believed for it. Then if there was no manifestation, they thought, "Well, the power is not here." They'd start singing, "Oh, Lord, send the power just now."

Because they couldn't see the anointing or feel it in manifestation, they thought it wasn't there. But the power of God is always present everywhere. God didn't leave most of His power over in one state and then leave only a little bit of it wherever you are! No, wherever God is, *all* of His ability, *all* of His power, and *all* of His capabilities are present.

So you can see, it's not a matter of the power getting the job done by itself. No, a person must appropriate or activate the power for himself for it to work for him.

Certainly, it's true that it's "not by might, nor by power, but by My Spirit, saith the Lord" (Zech. 4:6). But we've still got to *cooperate* with God's Spirit by believing in Him if we want to get the blessing. We've got to learn to mix faith *with* the power.

Let's look at Acts chapter 6, and you'll see that what I'm saying is exactly proven by God's Word.

ACTS 6:3–6

3   Wherefore, brethren, look ye out among you seven men of honest
    report, full of the Holy Ghost and wisdom, whom we may appoint
    over this business.

4 But we will give ourselves continually to prayer, and to the ministry of the word.

5 And the saying pleased the whole multitude: and they chose Stephen, a man full of FAITH AND OF THE HOLY GHOST, and
   Philip, and Prochorus, and Nicanor, and Timon, and Parmenas,
   and Nicolas a proselyte of Antioch:

6 Whom they set before the apostles: and when they had prayed,
   they laid their hands on them.

Just to give you some background and history, here in Acts chapter 6 during the early days of the Church, the believers had "all things in common" (Acts 2:44). The disciples, the twelve apostles, were the only ministers those believers had at the beginning of the Early Church. It was a baby Church, just starting, and the Church didn't exist anywhere else except in Jerusalem at that time.

You see, Jesus had said to go into all the world and preach the Gospel to every creature (Mark 16:15). He'd also said in Acts 1:8 that *"after that the Holy Ghost is come upon you . . . ye shall be witnesses unto me both in Jerusalem, and in all Judaea, and in Samaria, and unto the uttermost part of the earth."* Yet, the believers hadn't witnessed anywhere except in Jerusalem.

So there in Jerusalem, the believers had all things in common, but some of them felt as if they were being neglected in the daily ministrations. So the Twelve said, *"Wherefore, brethren, look ye out among you seven men of HONEST REPORT, FULL OF THE HOLY GHOST and WISDOM, whom we may appoint over this business"* (Acts 6:3).

The men they were looking for had to meet three requirements: 1) have an honest report; 2) be full of the Holy Ghost; *and* 3) be full of wisdom.

You see, some people can be full of the Holy Ghost and yet not have much wisdom. Well, it wouldn't be wise to put them in charge of the handling of money. Then some folks may be full of the Holy Ghost and not have an honest report. It wouldn't be wise to put them over handling money either since they don't have an honest report.

So you'd want all three of these qualities in someone you'd appoint to oversee business matters—someone with *an honest report* and someone who was *full of the Holy Ghost* and *full of wisdom.*

You know, it's just not good for preachers to try to handle business affairs, because most preachers are not very good businessmen. God didn't call them to be businessmen; He called them to be preachers. And they'll usually make a mess trying to be businessmen.

As for a pastor, he has the spiritual oversight of a flock, but not necessarily the business oversight. That was the case in Acts chapter 6 concerning the Early Church.

ACTS 6:4

4 But we [the twelve apostles] will give ourselves continually to prayer, and to the ministry of the word.

I've seen many a pastoral ministry ruined because pastors spent all of their time on the business part of the church, and prayer and the Word was neglected. Their spiritual life just became a disaster. That'll happen every time, sooner or later, when prayer and the Word are neglected.

ACTS 6:3-5

3 Wherefore, brethren, look ye out among you seven men of honest report, full of the Holy Ghost and wisdom, whom we may appoint over this business.

4 But we will give ourselves continually to prayer, and to the ministry of the word.

5 And the saying pleased the whole multitude: and they chose Stephen, a man full of faith AND of the Holy Ghost . . . .

Verse 5 goes on to list seven men who were chosen to oversee the daily ministrations. Now all seven of these men were full of the Holy Ghost. That was one of the qualifications—that they be full of the Holy Ghost. But it says about Stephen that he was full of faith *and* the Holy Ghost or power. And there were certain miracles and signs that followed Stephen's mix of faith and power.

ACTS 6:8

8 And Stephen, full of faith and power, did great wonders and miracles among the people.

You see, if you are full of the Holy Ghost, you're full of power. I mean, you've got the Powerhouse in you! Well, every one of those seven men were full of power. But that doesn't mean that every one of them was full of faith.

Did you ever stop to think about the fact that every Spirit-filled believer—every believer who maintains the Spirit-filled experience—is full of power. He doesn't have to *get* full; he *is* full.

EPHESIANS 5:18

18 And be not drunk with wine, wherein is excess; but be [being] filled [or be continually filled] with the Spirit.

The Holy Ghost through the Apostle Paul was encouraging the Church at Ephesus to be filled with the Holy Spirit. You understand that the New Testament was originally written in Greek, and scholars tell us that in the Greek language, the phrase "be filled" in this verse denotes continuous action. A more literal translation is, "But be *being* filled with the Spirit."

Well, in the natural, you know how a fellow gets full of wine, don't you? He keeps on drinking. How can you tell when he gets full? Well, when he gets full, he does something. He starts acting *drunk!*

So Ephesians 5:18 tells you to be filled with the Spirit. How can you tell when you get filled? Acts 2:4 tells us: *"And they were all FILLED with the Holy Ghost, and BEGAN TO SPEAK with other tongues, as the Spirit gave them utterance."*

EPHESIANS 5:18-19

18 . . . be filled with the Spirit;

19 SPEAKING to yourselves in psalms and hymns and spiritual songs, singing and making melody in your heart to the Lord.

Now to be filled with the Spirit is to be filled with power. Jesus said in Acts 1:8, *"But ye shall receive POWER, after that the HOLY GHOST is come upon you."*

So we read in Acts 6:3 that the apostles said, *"look ye out among you seven men of honest report, FULL OF THE HOLY GHOST* [power] *and wisdom, whom we may appoint over this business."*

Power Alone Won't Get the Job Done—Your Faith Must Give Action to the Power!

All seven men listed in Acts 6:5 were full of the Holy Ghost. That means that all seven of these men were full of *power*. But apparently, there was only one of them who did any miracles and signs among the people, and that was Stephen.

Every one of them had the power to do the miracles and signs. Why didn't they do them then? *Because it takes faith to give action to the power!*

You can see where we as Full Gospel people and Pentecostal people, particularly in days gone by, have missed it. We've thought that if we had the power, the miracles and the wonders would just automatically follow.

But they won't. We saw that in Acts chapter 6. All seven of those men were full of power, but only one of them did any miracles or wonders, and that was Stephen. And Stephen wasn't even one of the Twelve. He wasn't a preacher or an apostle or an evangelist. In fact, he never did become an evangelist or an apostle or pastor; he lived and died a deacon.

ACTS 6:8

8 And Stephen, full of faith and power, did great wonders and miracles among the people.

Stephen didn't do great wonders and miracles just by being full of power. No, he was full of faith *and* power. And so we know that power by itself won't get the job done. You have to mix faith *with* the power to get the power to work.

Did you notice that the same thing is true in the case of an individual's healing? For example, in the case of the woman with the issue of blood, Jesus knew immediately that power had gone out of Him. But He didn't say, "Daughter, My *power* hath made thee whole." No, He said, "Daughter, thy *faith* hath made thee whole." It was her faith mixed with the power that healed her.

Also, did you notice that when Jesus and His disciples crossed over the sea of Galilee to the land of Gennesaret in Matthew 14, the people of that place "had knowledge of Jesus" and brought the sick and diseased to Him. And as the sick and the diseased touched the hem of Jesus' garment, they were made whole (vv. 35, 36).

But notice the men of Gennesaret did that *when* they "had knowledge of Him." They had to have heard about Jesus to have knowledge of Him. Well, we know that "faith comes by hearing, and hearing by the Word of God" (Rom. 10:17). So again, faith was involved.

Then in Luke chapter 6, it says the multitude came to hear Jesus and to be healed of their diseases. It said they sought to touch Jesus for there went virtue or power out of Him and healed them all. But notice they came to *hear* and to be healed. They heard first, and faith came. Then they sought to touch Him.

People need to understand about the healing anointing. They need to know that it exists, but just as importantly, they need to know how to get that anointing to work and produce results in their lives. They need to believe or have faith in the healing power of God.

I sometimes tell a story about Smith Wigglesworth in connection with the healing power or anointing. After Wigglesworth was here in America for a while and went back to England, a woman who'd discovered that she had cancer sent a handkerchief to Wigglesworth for him to lay hands on.

This woman who'd become bedfast knew that Wigglesworth was anointed, so she had her sister send the handkerchief.

Wigglesworth laid hands on the handkerchief and returned it to the sister. His instructions were to have all the believers in the family gather around the sick woman's bed, lay the handkerchief on her, and claim her healing.

Well, the sister laid the handkerchief on the pillow by the sick woman's head and went to round up the rest of the family to pray. While she was rounding up the rest of the family, she heard somebody shouting and jumping up and down and dancing in the front bedroom where her sister was. But she just knew it couldn't be her sister, because her sister was bedfast—she couldn't get out of bed!

So the family rushed to the front bedroom, and there was the sister, out of the bed, jumping up and down and hollering, "I'm healed! I'm healed! I'm healed!" The family didn't even get to do any praying!

They all shouted and rejoiced with the healed woman. Finally, when they all quieted down, they asked her, "What happened?"

"Well," she said to her sister, "you laid that handkerchief right there on the pillow by my head."

"Yes," her sister nodded.

"Well, you hardly got out of the room when I began to feel something coming out of that handkerchief into the side of my head."

"What did it feel like?" they all asked.

She said, "It was like a warm 'glow.' It came out of that handkerchief into my head and went all over my body and out the end of my toes. When it did, I was healed!"

Well, what was that warm glow? It was the anointing Wigglesworth was anointed with. He laid his hands on that handkerchief, and the cloth became saturated with that power!

Now the power didn't just flow out into that woman automatically. The woman evidently had faith. Her actions proved it—why else would she send for a handkerchief? She had to have believed in the healing power and that Wigglesworth was anointed with that power.

You see, a person's faith has something to do with healing even if the healing anointing is present and in manifestation.

You remember I said that Jesus ministered with and without the healing anointing in His earth walk. We said that sometimes there was a transfer of power from Jesus to the person He was ministering to, and sometimes there was no transfer of power. But in every case, the person receiving healing had to use faith to receive the desired result—healing.

FAITH BRINGS THE VICTORY!

Many years ago, one of the members of a church I pastored brought me a letter on a Sunday night. The church member said, "I live on the same street as this lady who's been bedfast for over two years. Her family is one of the leading families in the city. Her husband's been dead a good many years, and she is in her seventies. I didn't read this letter, but it's from this same lady. I think she wants you to come pray for her."

I opened the letter and read it. And sure enough, the letter said, "Dear Reverend Hagin. I don't know you, and you don't know me. I only know you from the newspaper account that you've come to pastor the Full Gospel church here. I know your church believes in divine healing, so I want you to come to my house tomorrow morning at ten o'clock to anoint me with oil and lay hands on me that I may be healed."

At ten o'clock the next morning, I stood on the porch at this woman's house, knocking at the front door.

A maid opened the door. I said, "I'm Reverend Hagin."

She said, "Yes. We're expecting you." She escorted me down a hall, knocked on a door, and a nurse in a white uniform opened the door. The nurse ushered me into the room, and there was the lady who'd sent the letter. She was a white-haired lady, seventy-seven years old. She was lying on a hospital bed that was cranked so she could sit up, sort of in a reclining position.

She had been bedfast for two years with a special nurse there with her at all times. The family was quite wealthy; they were leaders of the city.

I walked with the nurse to the woman's bedside, and the nurse introduced us. I took the woman's hand to shake hands with her. She said, "Brother Hagin, I'm too old to mince words. I'll just tell you why I sent for you.

"I belong to the First Such-and-such Church," and she named the church where she was a member. "I didn't send for anybody there, because they don't have any healing there—they don't believe in divine healing. But in years gone by I attended some services out at the Full Gospel church you pastor, and I saw them anointing people with oil and laying hands on them. I looked it up in the Scripture, and it's all in there. Now I just believe that if you'll anoint me with oil and lay hands on me, I'll be healed."

You see, this woman was believing something!

Well, up till the time she said in effect, "Brother Hagin, you just lay your hands on me and I'll be healed," I was wondering what the woman believed about healing. I went to that house wondering, "This lady's not a member of our congregation. I don't know her. Maybe I'll get to talk to her and get her saved. And maybe, eventually, I could possibly get her healed." I just didn't know for sure.

But then after she said all that, I saw that she was ready. I didn't hardly get my hand laid on her forehead to anoint her with oil when she was healed! She took the healing by her faith.

The following Sunday night, this seventy-seven-year-old woman and her daughter were in our church. The woman had been bedfast for more than two years. But then she was perfectly healed and in church!

Well, you see, it was her faith that healed her!

It was faith in the healing anointing that healed the bedridden sister who sent for a handkerchief from Smith Wigglesworth. You see, in both of these cases, the sick person expected to receive something—healing!

In the case of the woman who sent for the anointed handkerchief, it was her faith that caused the power in the handkerchief to be activated. Faith activated the power, and healing was the result!

THE VITAL IMPORTANCE OF POWER AND FAITH

Remember there were two important factors that brought about the result in the case of the woman with the issue of blood: power and faith. They go together just like a hand in a glove. We could say it like this: *Power is not active until faith is exercised.*

You know, I've been studying divine healing for more than sixty years. And to tell you the truth about the matter, I've come to find out that after sixty years, I still know very little about the subject.

I know when we're young, we begin to study a certain subject, and we think by the following Tuesday that we've learned all there is on that subject! We think we've become an authority on it!

But I have found that the more you learn, the less you find you really know. But one thing is clear to the student of divine healing: Sometimes, the healing power of God is ministered to a sick person so that the person is manifestly supercharged with heavenly electricity. *Yet no real or final healing takes place until something occurs that releases the faith of the individual.*

MY OWN EXPERIENCE

Back when I was healed as a teenager, I knew nothing about the power of God. I'd never felt anything in the way of the anointing. I knew on the inside of me that I was born again, all right, but my body was still paralyzed. I still had a heart condition. When I was born again, I had been bedfast for sixteen months, and I was still bedfast. I acted with no inspiration and no feeling on Mark 11:24 just as you'd "act" on the multiplication table, believing that two times two equals four!

I just read that scripture, Mark 11:24, *"What things soever ye desire, when ye pray, believe that ye receive them, and ye shall have them."*

When I started acting on that verse, I didn't feel anything. In fact, I never felt less religious in my life! I never felt so dull and dry.

I didn't know you were supposed to feel anything special or out of the ordinary (some people think that if they don't have some special feeling, they didn't get their answer). In the denomination I was in, we didn't have any tangible anointing! So I wasn't looking to feel anything. I was just acting on the scripture because it was God's Word.

I began to act upon the Word and say, "Now according to Mark 11:24, 'When you pray, believe you receive, and you shall have it,' I believe I receive my healing."

So I started saying out loud, "I believe I receive my healing. I believe I receive healing for the deformed heart. I believe I receive healing for the paralysis. I believe I receive healing for the incurable blood disease."

Then an inward voice, just a still small voice on the inside of me, said, "Now you believe that you are well." It was the inward voice of the Holy Spirit in my spirit.

I said, "I sure do believe I'm well."

Here's where folks get mixed up on this believing or faith business. They'll say, "Well, I'd confess that, but I'm not well!"

But there's a difference between *believing what you see and feel* and *believing what God says in His Word*.

You see, I didn't confess that I believed I was well because I *felt* well. If I would have done that, I would have been lying. I didn't say I was well because I *looked* well. If I would have done that, I would have been lying. No, I said I believed I was well because I was *acting on the Word*!

—250—

And so that inward voice said, "Now you believe you are well." It didn't say, "You are well." It said, "You believe you are." And I said, "I sure do."

That inward voice said, "Get up then. Well people ought to be up at 10:30 in the morning." And ordinarily, that would be the case. Well people *would* be up at 10:30 in the morning.

You know, when the Holy Spirit said that, the thought crossed my mind, "How am I going to get up? Paralyzed people can't walk." But I struggled to get up and still never felt a thing. Then as I continued to make the effort to get up, I regained some use, probably two-thirds, of the upper part of my body.

I struggled to push myself to a seated position. I still never felt a thing. But then as I continued to struggle and act on the Word, I felt something come down over me. That's the first time I felt anything. It was like a warm glow or a warmth of some kind. It seemed as if it were striking me in the top of the head—as if somebody were standing over me, pouring honey or molasses on my head. It just "oozed" down over me.

That warmth went down over my head, my shoulders, my arms, my body, and out the end of my toes. Then I was standing straight, and the paralysis was gone! My heart condition was gone! And I've been healed ever since!

JUST BELIEVE YOU RECEIVE!

Some people think, "Well, I've got to get to Brother Hagin or somebody who's specially anointed to lay hands on me to be healed." And God does do that to help people who are on a lower level of faith. But, really, you don't have to have somebody who's specially anointed to lay hands on you.

When I was healed, I was healed with the same power — the same anointing—that God anoints certain people with. I didn't know of anybody who was anointed with that power to get to come and pray for me. Yet that same anointing was in my room. The Holy Ghost was there!

You don't have to have a special anointing to receive healing, because the Holy Spirit is there! It's the same anointing, the same Spirit, that oozed over my body like a warm glow when I acted on my faith. That same anointing that made me well!

But what caused the power or anointing to be activated that day? *My faith!* That power was there all the time, every single day. But it never was activated *until* I exercised faith!

Well, after I started preaching, I would teach people faith. Once in a while, we'd have manifestations of the Spirit or the anointing, and folks would receive healing as a result of their faith mixed with the power of God. But I'd get a lot of people healed when we didn't feel anything. We just believed, and it happened!

Yet, right on the other hand, even back then, people I'd pray for would say sometimes, "Something's all over me!" Well, I knew they were talking about the same thing that happened to me when I was healed. And those people were healed, because He was present! That same Spirit was present, and they mixed faith with the power and were healed!

Now I want to show you something about mixing faith with the power to receive healing. I tell this story sometimes, and the way I've told it in times past is quite humorous, but I'm going to tell it so it won't be so humorous and you'll get my point.

The thing that brought me around Pentecostal people was the fact that they believed in healing. I would get in their crowd to have some fellowship around faith and healing. But they taught that you could be baptized in the Holy Ghost and could speak with other tongues. I thought at first that they were in error. I didn't argue and fuss with them. I just said to myself, "Well, I'll put up with a little fanaticism and excess so I can have a little fellowship around faith and healing."

But it was sort of like a fellow in east Texas once said, "It's like a slippery creek bank. You keep fooling around it, and you'll slip in!" So I slipped in and got baptized with the Holy Ghost, speaking with other tongues, and I received the left foot of fellowship from among the denomination I'd been in.

That was 1937. Then in June 1939, my wife and I accepted the pastorate of a little Full Gospel church in the blacklands of north-central Texas.

Now both as a young Baptist boy pastor and then as a Full Gospel pastor, I'd always carry a little bottle of oil in my pocket. It was a small perfume bottle, actually, no longer than a key, that had olive oil in it. And I'd anoint people and lay hands on them, and they'd get healed.

That's right in keeping with James 5:14 and 15, which says, *"Is any sick among you? let him call for the elders of the church; and let them pray over him, anointing him with oil in the name of the Lord: And the prayer of faith shall save the sick, and the Lord shall raise him up; and if he have committed sins, they shall be forgiven him."*

Well, my wife and I were in the parsonage of our Full Gospel church one day, straightening up what little belongings we had. We'd only been married about six months. We didn't have any furniture except for one table, one chair, and a wooden apple crate. My wife would sit in the chair, and I'd sit on the apple box.

Boy, we started off big, didn't we! We didn't even have knives and forks to go around for the whole family, and there were only two of us! We didn't have enough cups and saucers to go around. We had cups with the handles knocked off. Some of the fine church members brought them to us and said, "We couldn't use them and thought that maybe you could." That's absolutely the truth!

Anyway, as we were straightening up what little things we had, there was a knock on the parsonage door. I opened it and there was a cotton-headed little boy about seven or eight years old.

Do you know what I mean by cotton-headed? His hair was blond. Really, it was so blond, it could have been platinum or white. His hair was just as white as cotton. My hair was just about that white until I was about twelve years old. Then it started getting darker through the years.

When I answered the door, this little fellow just blurted out, "Momma wants you to come pray for her!"

I said, "Who?"

"She's sick," he said.

I said, "Well, who's Momma?" I didn't even know who *he* was, much less who *Momma* was.

He said, "Sister S_____," and he called out her name.

When he said her name, I recognized that she was one of the Sunday school teachers in the church. I said, "Son, stand right here until I put my tie and coat on, and I'll let you show me the way to your house." So he waited.

When I arrived at their house, there was his mother, sick in bed. I got that little bottle of oil out, took the top off, dabbed a little oil on my finger, and anointed her forehead. Then I knelt by the bed and prayed. Afterward, I got up and said, "Amen." I put the bottle of anointing oil back in my pocket and started to leave.

PRAYING THE POWER DOWN

As I turned to leave, the woman said, "Wait, Brother Hagin." Then, calling out the name of the former pastor, she said, "Brother B_____ always prayed until the power fell." Evidently, he'd been praying for her healing too.

Well, I was new in Pentecostal circles. I'd just come out of a denominational church. I did know enough to know that the power does fall. And, you see, prayer will bring that power into manifestation.

I knew that the power of God does fall like rain. In fact, the Bible calls it the early and latter rain (James 5:7). Hosea prophesied that the Lord will come unto us as the rain (Hosea 6:3). And the Bible talks about Peter's preaching at Cornelius' household and the Spirit of God falling on all of them there (Acts 10:44).

ACTS 10:42–45

42 And he commanded us to preach unto the people, and to testify that it is he which was ordained of God to be the Judge of quick and dead.

43 To him give all the prophets witness, that through his name whosoever believeth in him shall receive remission of sins.

44 While Peter yet spake these words, the Holy Ghost FELL on all them which heard the word.

45 And they of the circumcision which believed were astonished, as many as came with Peter, because that on the Gentiles also was POURED OUT the gift of the Holy Ghost.

The Scripture says the Holy Ghost *fell* on those of Cornelius' household. Then it says in verse 45 that the Holy Ghost was *poured out*.

Well, rain or water falls or it can be poured out. And sometimes we liken an outpouring of the Spirit of God to rain falling or to water being poured out. So I knew that the power did fall.

When that woman said, "Brother B_____ always prayed until the power fell," I got back down on my knees, thinking, "Well, I'm a Full Gospel preacher now. I guess that's the way they do it here."

So I prayed for about an hour and a half. That's how long it took me to pray the power into *manifestation*, because, you see, it was there *present* the whole time. But those people thought the power wasn't present if it wasn't manifested. So it took about an hour and a half to get it into manifestation. (I eventually got "expert" at it, and I could do it much quicker.)

So after an hour and a half of praying, the power fell. It was just like rain falling on us in that room. The Holy Ghost power of God fell. The woman shook, the bed shook, and the house shook. And it was a clear day outside!

Well, all through the summer, I'd have to go at least twice a week and pray the power of God down on that woman. She never did get healed, but I prayed the power down on her many times!

I started praying for this woman in June. In August of that same year, I prayed the power down on her one particular time until, God as my witness, the windows rattled in that bedroom like there was a storm on! It was on a clear day in August with maybe one or two cumulus clouds in the sky.

There wasn't a leaf stirring outside. Yet when the power of God came on that woman, she shook until she nearly shook right off the bed. But she never did get healed. Each time I prayed for her, she'd think she was healed only when she felt the power. When she didn't feel the power anymore, she thought she wasn't healed.

One day at about two o'clock in the afternoon, I heard a knock at my door. It was that same little cotton-headed boy. He said, "Momma wants you to come pray for her."

Now I'd already prayed for his momma once that day. I said to the boy, "I thought she got healed this morning."

He said, "She did, but she's worse now."

So I went back down to their house and prayed until I prayed the power down. She shook, the bed shook, and the house shook, and I went home.

The next morning at about 10:15 a.m., there was a knock on the door. I went to the door, and there stood that little boy. "Momma wants you to come pray for her."

I said, "I thought she got healed twice yesterday."

He said, "She did, but she's worse today. She's hurting awfully bad."

"Well," I said, "all right. I'll be down there in a few minutes." So I put on my tie and my coat and went down to their house. I anointed her with oil and prayed until I prayed the power down. The power fell down on her; she shook, the bed shook, the house shook, the windows rattled, and I went home.

Sometime later that day, in the middle of the afternoon, there was a knock on the door. I went to the door, and there stood that little boy!

I said, "I know. I know. Your momma wants me to come pray for her."

Then I said, "I thought she got healed three times already."

He said, "She did, but she's hurting worse and wants you to come and pray for her."

Well, as I said, that continued all summer. I wasn't going over there every day, but I was going over there at least two or three times a week. That was in 1939.

LEARN TO TAKE GOD AT HIS WORD

Let's skip over to '41, '42, and on over to 1943. I was still going down to that woman's house, praying the power down on her, and she was still not healed! Yes, she'd get temporary relief, and she'd be in church for a while. But then the temporary relief she received would wear off, and she'd be back down again. It just went on and on and on.

Later we built a couple of rooms onto the parsonage, so I was working kind of late, wallpapering the rooms and doing some finishing work. Some of the men of the church were carpenters and had done most of the building, but I was just finishing it out and putting down some baseboards and so forth.

We were in a revival and had a guest evangelist in doing the speaking. I had been working extra late on those new rooms so I wouldn't have to work on them the following day. Folks were already arriving for the meeting, and I was running a little late getting ready for the meeting.

I heard my wife let somebody in the front door, and I heard her say, "He's back there working in the bathroom." I looked up, and here came that little cotton-headed boy.

Well, this little boy and I had worked together for almost four years, so I could practically read his mind!

He never said anything. I said, "Yes, I know. Your momma wants me to come pray for her."

It was ten minutes until time to start church. Well, how in the world was I going to get in all that praying I'd been doing in only ten minutes? I started to say, "Would it be all right to wait until after church?" but all I got out of my mouth was "Would . . . ," and the boy said, "No. She said to come on right now before church. She's hurting awfully bad."

You see, this boy and I had worked together so long that we knew what the other was going to say! The only difference was, he was nine years old by then (he was still cotton-headed).

I said, "Well, all right then." So I shaved, jumped into my meeting clothes, and ran out the back door.

I had a car sitting right by the back door of the parsonage. But if I would have gone by car, it would have taken me longer to get there. So I ran out the back door of the parsonage and down an alley. I ran up another alley, across another street, and up another alley before I reached her house. I knocked on the side door and a voice said, "Come in." By the time I got inside, I already had the top off of that bottle of oil!

I was out of breath from running. I just anointed her head with oil and said, "Oh, God, heal this woman in the Name of Jesus.

You said if we ask it in Your Name, You'd do it, so You've done it. Amen."

By the time I said "Amen," I had the top back on the bottle and was headed for the door. I started to open the door, and this woman started to say something. But I'd worked with her so long, almost four years, that I knew what she was going to say.

I don't know how come I say some of the things I say. I mean, some of the things I say surprise me as much as anybody else. But when this woman started to say something, I turned to her and said, "I know. I know. You're hurting worse now than you were when I came in the door a few seconds ago.

"But Jesus said if we'd ask in His Name, He'd do it. So He's done it. That's it; it's settled. The next time you see me, you'll tell me it's so. Good-bye."

Then I ran out the door, down one alley, across a street, down another alley and then another until I reached the church. I came in the church door, out of breath. I looked at my watch, and it was exactly time for church to start!

Well, I got up in the pulpit. I didn't even have to get warmed up; I was *already* warmed up! And we started the service.

We went through all the preliminaries—praise and worship, special songs, and the offering—in about forty-five minutes. Then I said, "Before Brother R_____ comes to preach, let's have one person from each of these three sections who's been saved during these meetings to stand up and testify." (You know, it's good for people who've just been saved to get up and tell about it. It strengthens them.)

So one person got up and testified. Then another person got up and testified. And about the time the third person got up and started testifying, the double doors at the back of the auditorium burst open, and in came the woman I'd just prayed for.

Well, I guess she thought we were having a testimony meeting, because when the third person sat down, she just picked up giving her own testimony as she walked up the aisle.

She said, "Brother Hagin, I'm perfectly healed, just like you said. After you anointed me with oil and prayed, I started hurting twice as bad as I was hurting before. That's what I was going to say when you started to leave. But you said, 'Sister, we prayed in the Name of Jesus. He said, "If you ask in My Name, I'll do it." So He's done it. The next time you see me, you'll tell me it's so.'"

She continued, "You weren't gone ten minutes when every symptom left me, and I got up and got ready and came to church!"

Now we'd spent four years praying the power down, feeling the power, shaking under the power, and falling under the power (and all that's all right if you mix faith with it). But, you see, the power of God had surcharged that woman again and again and again. Yet no real and final healing ever occurred *until* something happened to release the woman's faith.

You see, what I said to her that last time I prayed for her caused her to release her faith. And I never did have to go pray for her like that anymore. She was healed of that chronic condition. If there was ever anything else wrong with her, she'd come on to church to be prayed for there. She'd say, "Brother Hagin, I know the minute you touch me in Jesus' Name, I'll be healed." And she was!

There was a flu epidemic going around once after that, and this woman was so sick she couldn't get up. So we did go pray for her then. But that was it. All that running and praying stopped. She learned how to release her faith!

That's the reason I said to you that although the healing power may be ministered to a person, and though that person may manifestly be supercharged with the power of God, no real and final healing takes place until something occurs that releases the faith of the individual.

The Bible said in Hebrews 4:2, *"For unto us was the gospel preached, as well as unto them* [talking about Israel]: *but the word preached did not profit them, NOT BEING MIXED WITH FAITH in them that heard it."*

Friends, you'll not get any healing from Heaven if you do not believe that there's any for you. You'll never get it applied to your circumstances so that it will do you any good *until* you lay hold of it intelligently and receive it!

One way to receive the healing power, of course, is through the laying on of hands. Or you could receive it from a cloth or a handkerchief that has absorbed the anointing. On the other hand, receiving healing that way is only *one* way to receive.

—263—

Receiving healing through the healing anointing is not the only way to receive healing. Remember I said you could receive healing by acting in simple faith on the Word like I did.

Also, in every service we hold, the Holy Ghost is there. And since the Holy Ghost is there, He is present with all the power He has! You can just receive your need met by faith. You can mix your faith with the power that's present, whether the power is in manifestation or not.

You Can Receive Power From Heaven To Change Your Circumstances

In conclusion, let's sum up a few things about the healing power of God. When we understand some things about the anointing, we can appropriate it for ourselves and reap the benefit of this power in our own lives.

The healing anointing is a tangible substance. And the Word of God reveals to us the rules and laws that govern its operation.

The Lord Jesus Christ revealed and applied the laws of the Spirit, which demonstrated the fact that the healing power of God is a tangible substance, a heavenly materiality.

Now you'll not receive any of this power from Heaven if you don't believe there's any there. If you don't believe it exists, you'll never get it applied to your circumstances so that it will do you any good. The healing power of God will not benefit you until you believe in it, lay hold of it intelligently by faith and simply receive it.

But, thank God, through your faith in the holy written Word and in the mighty power of God, you *can* receive divine healing! By believing what God's Word says about the healing anointing, you can enjoy all the blessings and benefits of this power from Heaven that is available to us today.